50 Ultra French Cake Recipes for Home

By: Kelly Johnson

Table of Contents

- Tarte Tatin
- Opéra Cake
- Madeleines
- Financiers
- Clafoutis
- Éclair au Chocolat
- Génoise
- Tarte au Citron
- Gâteau Basque
- Fraisier Cake
- Paris-Brest
- Mousse au Chocolat Cake
- Charlotte aux Fruits
- Battenberg Cake (French twist)
- Gâteau au Yaourt
- Mocha Cake
- Gâteau Saint-Honoré
- Pain d'Épices
- Baba au Rhum
- Gâteau de Crêpes
- Tarte aux Pommes
- Canelés
- Quatre-Quarts
- Tarte aux Fruits Rouges
- Tarte Bourdaloue
- Bûche de Noël
- Marquise au Chocolat
- Tarte au Chocolat
- Mille-Feuille
- Tarte aux Abricots
- Tartelette au Citron
- Gâteau aux Noix
- Crêpes Suzette Cake
- Parisienne Cake
- Tarte au Praliné
- Gâteau de Mamie

- Pithiviers
- Gâteau au Chocolat Moelleux
- Tarte aux Poires
- Kouign-Amann
- Gâteau aux Pommes
- Gâteau au Citron
- Tarte au Caramel
- Gâteau de Voyage
- Bûche Pralinée
- Gâteau Opéra
- Gâteau au Miel
- Tarte au Miel
- Tarte Normande
- Gâteau à la Crème

Tarte Tatin

Ingredients:

- **For the Caramel:**
    - 1 cup (200 g) granulated sugar
    - 1/4 cup (60 ml) water
    - 2 tablespoons unsalted butter
- **For the Filling:**
    - 6-8 medium apples (such as Granny Smith or Honeycrisp), peeled, cored, and cut into wedges
    - 1/2 teaspoon ground cinnamon (optional)
    - 1 tablespoon lemon juice
- **For the Pastry:**
    - 1 sheet of pre-made puff pastry or homemade pie dough
    - Flour, for dusting

Instructions:

1. **Preheat the Oven:**
    - Preheat your oven to 375°F (190°C).
2. **Make the Caramel:**
    - In a medium, heavy-bottomed skillet, combine the sugar and water. Cook over medium heat, without stirring, until the sugar dissolves and turns a deep amber color. This should take about 10 minutes.
    - Remove from heat and carefully stir in the butter until melted and combined. Be careful, as the caramel will bubble up.
3. **Prepare the Apples:**
    - Toss the apple wedges with lemon juice and cinnamon, if using.
4. **Assemble the Tarte Tatin:**
    - Pour the caramel into a 9-10 inch (23-25 cm) ovenproof skillet or a round cake pan.
    - Arrange the apple wedges in a tight, concentric pattern over the caramel, packing them in as they will shrink during cooking.
5. **Add the Pastry:**
    - Roll out the puff pastry or pie dough on a lightly floured surface to fit your skillet or pan.
    - Place the pastry over the apples, tucking the edges around the apples into the skillet.
6. **Bake:**
    - Bake in the preheated oven for 35-40 minutes, or until the pastry is golden brown and crispy.
7. **Cool and Serve:**

- Let the tart cool in the pan for 5 minutes. Carefully invert it onto a serving plate while still warm. If some apples stick to the pan, just place them back on the tart.

Enjoy your homemade Tarte Tatin! It's delicious served warm with a dollop of crème fraîche or vanilla ice cream.

Opéra Cake

Ingredients:

For the Coffee Syrup:

- 1/2 cup (120 ml) strong brewed coffee
- 1/4 cup (50 g) granulated sugar

For the Almond Sponge Cake (Génoise):

- 4 large eggs
- 1/2 cup (100 g) granulated sugar
- 1/2 cup (60 g) all-purpose flour
- 1/2 cup (50 g) almond flour
- 2 tablespoons unsalted butter, melted

For the Coffee Buttercream:

- 1 cup (230 g) unsalted butter, softened
- 2 cups (250 g) powdered sugar
- 2 tablespoons brewed coffee, cooled
- 1 teaspoon vanilla extract

For the Chocolate Ganache:

- 1 cup (240 ml) heavy cream
- 8 oz (225 g) dark chocolate, finely chopped
- 1 tablespoon unsalted butter

For the Assembly:

- 1 cup (240 ml) heavy cream, whipped to soft peaks

Instructions:

1. **Prepare the Coffee Syrup:**
    - Combine the brewed coffee and sugar in a saucepan. Heat until the sugar is dissolved. Let it cool.
2. **Make the Almond Sponge Cake:**
    - Preheat the oven to 350°F (175°C). Line a baking sheet with parchment paper.
    - Beat the eggs and sugar until thick and pale. Gently fold in the flour and almond flour. Stir in the melted butter.
    - Spread the batter evenly on the prepared baking sheet. Bake for 10-12 minutes. Let it cool completely.
3. **Prepare the Coffee Buttercream:**

- Beat the butter until creamy. Gradually add powdered sugar, mixing until smooth. Blend in the coffee and vanilla extract. Set aside.
4. **Make the Chocolate Ganache:**
    - Heat the cream until just boiling, then pour it over the chopped chocolate. Let it sit for 2 minutes, then stir until smooth. Stir in the butter. Let it cool until spreadable.
5. **Assemble the Cake:**
    - Cut the sponge cake into 3 equal rectangles.
    - Place one rectangle on a serving plate and brush with coffee syrup. Spread a layer of coffee buttercream over it.
    - Add the second rectangle of sponge cake and brush with coffee syrup. Spread a layer of chocolate ganache.
    - Top with the final sponge cake layer and brush with syrup. Spread a thin layer of ganache over the top and sides of the cake.
6. **Finish:**
    - Decorate the cake with whipped cream or additional ganache as desired.

Ch ll the cake before serving to allow the flavors to meld. Enjoy your Opéra Cake!

Madeleines

Ingredients:

- 1/2 cup (115 g) unsalted butter, plus extra for greasing
- 1 cup (120 g) all-purpose flour
- 1/2 cup (100 g) granulated sugar
- 2 large eggs
- 1 teaspoon vanilla extract
- 1/2 teaspoon baking powder
- A pinch of salt
- Zest of 1 lemon (optional)

Instructions:

1. **Prepare the Pan:**
   - Preheat your oven to 375°F (190°C). Grease a madeleine pan with butter and lightly dust with flour.
2. **Melt the Butter:**
   - Melt the butter and let it cool slightly.
3. **Mix the Batter:**
   - In a bowl, whisk together the eggs and sugar until light and frothy. Stir in the vanilla extract and lemon zest if using.
   - In another bowl, sift together the flour, baking powder, and salt.
   - Gently fold the dry ingredients into the egg mixture. Then fold in the melted butter until just combined.
4. **Fill the Pan:**
   - Spoon the batter into the madeleine pan, filling each mold about 3/4 full.
5. **Bake:**
   - Bake for 10-12 minutes, or until the madeleines are golden brown and have a slight dome shape.
6. **Cool:**
   - Remove from the oven and let cool in the pan for a few minutes, then transfer to a wire rack to cool completely.

Enjoy these light, buttery treats with a cup of tea!

Financiers

Ingredients:

- 1/2 cup (115 g) unsalted butter
- 1 cup (100 g) almond flour
- 1 cup (125 g) powdered sugar
- 1/4 cup (30 g) all-purpose flour
- 4 large egg whites
- 1/4 teaspoon salt
- 1/2 teaspoon vanilla extract

Instructions:

1. **Prepare the Butter:**
   - Melt the butter in a saucepan until it turns a golden brown color. Let it cool slightly.
2. **Mix Dry Ingredients:**
   - In a bowl, combine the almond flour, powdered sugar, and all-purpose flour.
3. **Whip Egg Whites:**
   - In another bowl, beat the egg whites with salt until foamy but not stiff.
4. **Combine Ingredients:**
   - Gently fold the dry ingredients into the egg whites. Then fold in the melted butter and vanilla extract until just combined.
5. **Prepare the Pan:**
   - Preheat your oven to 375°F (190°C). Grease financier molds or line with parchment paper.
6. **Bake:**
   - Spoon the batter into the molds, filling each about 3/4 full. Bake for 15-20 minutes, or until the tops are golden brown and a toothpick inserted comes out clean.
7. **Cool:**
   - Allow the financiers to cool in the pan for a few minutes, then transfer to a wire rack to cool completely.

These are perfect with coffee or tea. Enjoy!

Clafoutis

Ingredients:

- 1 cup (240 ml) whole milk
- 3 large eggs
- 1 cup (100 g) granulated sugar
- 1/2 teaspoon vanilla extract
- 1/4 teaspoon salt
- 1/2 cup (60 g) all-purpose flour
- 2 tablespoons unsalted butter, melted
- 2 cups (250 g) pitted cherries (or other fruit of choice)
- Powdered sugar for dusting (optional)

Instructions:

1. **Preheat Oven:**
    - Preheat your oven to 350°F (175°C). Butter a 9-inch (23 cm) pie dish or similar baking dish.
2. **Prepare the Batter:**
    - In a blender or mixing bowl, combine the milk, eggs, sugar, vanilla extract, and salt. Blend or whisk until smooth.
    - Gradually add the flour, mixing until just combined. Stir in the melted butter.
3. **Assemble:**
    - Pour a small amount of batter into the prepared dish and bake for 5 minutes, just to set the base slightly.
    - Remove from the oven and scatter the cherries evenly over the partially baked batter.
4. **Bake:**
    - Pour the remaining batter over the cherries and bake for 35-40 minutes, or until the clafoutis is puffed and golden brown. A knife inserted should come out clean.
5. **Cool:**
    - Allow to cool slightly before dusting with powdered sugar, if desired.

Enjoy this classic French dessert warm or at room temperature!

Éclair au Chocolat

Ingredients:

For the Choux Pastry:

- 1/2 cup (115 g) unsalted butter
- 1 cup (240 ml) water
- 1/4 teaspoon salt
- 1 cup (125 g) all-purpose flour
- 4 large eggs

For the Chocolate Pastry Cream:

- 2 cups (480 ml) whole milk
- 1/2 cup (100 g) granulated sugar
- 1/4 cup (25 g) unsweetened cocoa powder
- 1/4 cup (30 g) cornstarch
- 4 large egg yolks
- 2 tablespoons unsalted butter
- 1 teaspoon vanilla extract

For the Chocolate Glaze:

- 4 oz (115 g) dark chocolate, finely chopped
- 1/2 cup (120 ml) heavy cream
- 1 tablespoon unsalted butter

Instructions:

1. Prepare the Choux Pastry:

- Preheat your oven to 400°F (200°C). Line a baking sheet with parchment paper.
- In a medium saucepan, combine the butter, water, and salt. Bring to a boil over medium heat.
- Once boiling, remove from heat and quickly stir in the flour. Return to heat and cook, stirring constantly, until the dough forms a smooth ball and pulls away from the sides of the pan.
- Transfer the dough to a bowl and let it cool for a few minutes. Once cool, beat in the eggs one at a time, ensuring each egg is fully incorporated before adding the next.
- Transfer the dough to a piping bag fitted with a large round tip. Pipe 4-inch (10 cm) lengths of dough onto the prepared baking sheet, spacing them about 2 inches apart.
- Bake for 20-25 minutes, or until golden brown and puffed. Let cool completely on a wire rack.

2. Make the Chocolate Pastry Cream:

- In a medium saucepan, heat the milk until just boiling.
- In a bowl, whisk together the sugar, cocoa powder, cornstarch, and egg yolks until smooth.
- Gradually whisk the hot milk into the egg mixture. Return the mixture to the saucepan and cook over medium heat, whisking constantly, until thickened and bubbling.
- Remove from heat and whisk in the butter and vanilla extract. Let the pastry cream cool to room temperature, then cover and refrigerate until set.

3. Prepare the Chocolate Glaze:

- In a small saucepan, heat the cream until just boiling. Pour over the chopped chocolate in a bowl. Let sit for 2 minutes, then stir until smooth. Stir in the butter until fully incorporated.

4. Assemble the Éclairs:

- Once the choux pastry is cool, use a serrated knife to cut them in half lengthwise.
- Fill the bottom halves with the chocolate pastry cream using a piping bag fitted with a star tip.
- Dip the top halves in the chocolate glaze or spread the glaze over them with a spoon. Place the glazed tops back on the filled bottoms.

5. Chill and Serve:

- Refrigerate the éclairs for at least 30 minutes to set the glaze before serving.

Enjoy your homemade éclairs au chocolat!

Génoise

Ingredients:

- 4 large eggs
- 1 cup (200 g) granulated sugar
- 1 cup (125 g) all-purpose flour
- 1/4 teaspoon salt
- 1/4 cup (60 g) unsalted butter, melted and cooled
- 1 teaspoon vanilla extract (optional)

Instructions:

1. **Preheat Oven:**
    - Preheat your oven to 350°F (175°C). Grease and flour an 8-inch (20 cm) round cake pan or line it with parchment paper.
2. **Prepare the Batter:**
    - In a large bowl, beat the eggs and sugar together with an electric mixer on high speed until thick and pale, about 5-7 minutes.
    - Sift the flour and salt together. Gently fold the flour mixture into the egg mixture, being careful not to deflate the batter.
    - Fold in the melted butter and vanilla extract until just combined.
3. **Bake:**
    - Pour the batter into the prepared pan and smooth the top. Bake for 25-30 minutes, or until the cake is golden and a toothpick inserted into the center comes out clean.
4. **Cool:**
    - Let the cake cool in the pan for 10 minutes, then transfer to a wire rack to cool completely.

Use this Génoise as a base for layered cakes or a simple sponge dessert. Enjoy!

Tarte au Citron

Ingredients:

For the Crust:

- 1 1/2 cups (190 g) all-purpose flour
- 1/2 cup (100 g) granulated sugar
- 1/4 teaspoon salt
- 1/2 cup (115 g) unsalted butter, cold and cut into cubes
- 1 large egg yolk
- 2-3 tablespoons ice water

For the Lemon Filling:

- 1 cup (240 ml) freshly squeezed lemon juice
- 1 cup (200 g) granulated sugar
- 4 large eggs
- 1/4 cup (60 ml) heavy cream
- 1/4 cup (60 g) unsalted butter, cut into small pieces
- Zest of 2 lemons

For the Meringue (optional):

- 3 large egg whites
- 1/2 cup (100 g) granulated sugar
- 1/4 teaspoon cream of tartar

Instructions:

1. Prepare the Crust:

- Preheat your oven to 375°F (190°C).
- In a food processor, combine the flour, sugar, and salt. Add the cold butter and pulse until the mixture resembles coarse crumbs.
- Add the egg yolk and pulse to combine. Gradually add ice water, 1 tablespoon at a time, until the dough comes together.
- Press the dough into the bottom and up the sides of a 9-inch (23 cm) tart pan. Prick the bottom with a fork.
- Bake for 15-20 minutes, or until lightly golden. Let cool.

2. Make the Lemon Filling:

- In a saucepan, whisk together the lemon juice, sugar, and eggs. Cook over medium heat, stirring constantly, until the mixture thickens and reaches 170°F (77°C).
- Remove from heat and stir in the heavy cream, butter, and lemon zest until smooth.

- Pour the lemon filling into the cooled tart crust and smooth the top. Bake for 15-20 minutes, or until the filling is just set but still slightly jiggly in the center. Let cool completely.

3. Make the Meringue (optional):

- Beat the egg whites and cream of tartar until soft peaks form. Gradually add the sugar and continue to beat until stiff, glossy peaks form.
- Spread or pipe the meringue over the cooled lemon filling. Use a kitchen torch or broiler to lightly brown the meringue, if desired.

Chill the tart before serving for the best flavor and texture. Enjoy your Tarte au Citron!

Gâteau Basque

Ingredients:

For the Dough:

- 1 1/2 cups (190 g) all-purpose flour
- 1/2 cup (100 g) granulated sugar
- 1/4 teaspoon salt
- 1/2 cup (115 g) unsalted butter, cold and cut into cubes
- 1 large egg yolk
- 1 large egg (for brushing)

For the Filling:

For the Almond Cream Filling:

- 1/2 cup (100 g) granulated sugar
- 1/2 cup (115 g) unsalted butter, softened
- 1 cup (100 g) almond flour
- 1 large egg
- 1 tablespoon all-purpose flour

For the Pastry Cream Filling:

- 1 cup (240 ml) whole milk
- 1/2 cup (100 g) granulated sugar
- 1/4 cup (25 g) cornstarch
- 2 large egg yolks
- 1 tablespoon unsalted butter
- 1 teaspoon vanilla extract

Instructions:

1. Prepare the Dough:

- In a large bowl or food processor, combine the flour, sugar, and salt. Add the cold butter and mix until the mixture resembles coarse crumbs.
- Add the egg yolk and mix until the dough comes together. If needed, add a little cold water, a teaspoon at a time, until the dough is cohesive.
- Divide the dough into two pieces, one slightly larger than the other. Flatten into discs, wrap in plastic, and refrigerate for at least 1 hour.

2. Make the Almond Cream Filling (if using):

- In a bowl, cream together the sugar and butter until light and fluffy. Stir in the almond flour, egg, and flour until smooth.

3. Make the Pastry Cream Filling:

- In a saucepan, heat the milk until it just begins to boil.
- In a separate bowl, whisk together the sugar, cornstarch, and egg yolks. Gradually whisk in the hot milk.
- Return the mixture to the saucepan and cook over medium heat, whisking constantly, until thickened and just boiling. Remove from heat and stir in the butter and vanilla extract. Cool to room temperature.

4. Assemble the Gâteau Basque:

- Preheat your oven to 375°F (190°C). Grease an 8-inch (20 cm) round cake pan or tart pan.
- Roll out the larger piece of dough on a floured surface to fit the bottom of your pan. Place it in the pan and press it into the sides.
- Spread the filling evenly over the dough. If using almond cream, spread it over the dough; if using pastry cream, spread that over the dough.
- Roll out the smaller piece of dough and place it over the filling. Trim any excess dough and press the edges to seal.
- Brush the top with a beaten egg for a golden finish. Use a fork to lightly score the top in a decorative pattern.

5. Bake:

- Bake for 35-40 minutes, or until the pastry is golden brown and the filling is set.
- Allow the cake to cool in the pan for about 10 minutes before transferring to a wire rack to cool completely.

Enjoy your Gâteau Basque, a delightful treat with a rich, buttery crust and flavorful filling!

Fraisier Cake

Ingredients:

For the Génoise Sponge Cake:

- 4 large eggs
- 1 cup (200 g) granulated sugar
- 1 cup (125 g) all-purpose flour
- 1/4 teaspoon salt
- 1/2 cup (115 g) unsalted butter, melted and cooled

For the Strawberry Cream Filling:

- 1 1/2 cups (360 ml) heavy cream
- 1/2 cup (60 g) powdered sugar
- 1 teaspoon vanilla extract
- 1 cup (250 g) strawberries, hulled and sliced
- 1/4 cup (60 ml) strawberry liqueur or syrup (optional)

For the Strawberry Glaze:

- 1/2 cup (120 ml) strawberry puree (fresh or from frozen strawberries)
- 1/4 cup (50 g) granulated sugar
- 1 tablespoon cornstarch
- 1 tablespoon lemon juice

Instructions:

1. Prepare the Génoise Sponge Cake:

- Preheat your oven to 350°F (175°C). Grease and flour two 8-inch (20 cm) round cake pans.
- In a large bowl, beat the eggs and sugar together until thick and pale. This should take about 5-7 minutes.
- Sift the flour and salt together. Gently fold into the egg mixture.
- Fold in the melted butter until just combined.
- Divide the batter evenly between the prepared pans and smooth the tops.
- Bake for 20-25 minutes, or until golden and a toothpick inserted into the center comes out clean. Let cool completely.

2. Prepare the Strawberry Cream Filling:

- In a mixing bowl, whip the heavy cream with powdered sugar and vanilla extract until stiff peaks form.

- Fold in the sliced strawberries. If desired, lightly brush the cooled cake layers with strawberry liqueur or syrup.

3. Assemble the Cake:

- Place one layer of the sponge cake on a serving plate or cake board. Spread a layer of the strawberry cream filling over it.
- Place the second cake layer on top and spread the remaining cream filling evenly over the top and sides.
- Chill in the refrigerator while you prepare the strawberry glaze.

4. Prepare the Strawberry Glaze:

- In a small saucepan, combine the strawberry puree, sugar, and cornstarch. Cook over medium heat, stirring constantly, until thickened.
- Remove from heat and stir in the lemon juice. Let it cool to room temperature.

5. Finish the Cake:

- Pour the strawberry glaze over the chilled cake, spreading it evenly.
- Chill the cake for at least 2 hours before serving to set the glaze.

Enjoy your Fraisier Cake, a delightful treat that showcases fresh strawberries and creamy filling!

Paris-Brest

Ingredients:

For the Choux Pastry:

- 1/2 cup (115 g) unsalted butter
- 1 cup (240 ml) water
- 1/4 teaspoon salt
- 1 cup (125 g) all-purpose flour
- 4 large eggs

For the Praline Cream Filling:

- 1 cup (240 ml) heavy cream
- 1/2 cup (125 g) praline paste (store-bought or homemade)
- 1/2 cup (100 g) powdered sugar

For the Almond Topping:

- 1/4 cup (30 g) sliced almonds
- 1 tablespoon granulated sugar (for sprinkling)

Instructions:

1. Prepare the Choux Pastry:

- Preheat your oven to 375°F (190°C). Line a baking sheet with parchment paper.
- In a medium saucepan, combine the butter, water, and salt. Bring to a boil over medium heat.
- Once boiling, remove from heat and quickly stir in the flour. Return to the heat and cook, stirring constantly, until the dough forms a smooth ball and pulls away from the sides of the pan.
- Transfer the dough to a mixing bowl and let it cool slightly. Add the eggs one at a time, beating well after each addition until fully incorporated and the dough is smooth.
- Transfer the dough to a piping bag fitted with a large round tip. Pipe a large ring of dough onto the prepared baking sheet, making a circle about 8 inches (20 cm) in diameter. Pipe a second smaller ring of dough inside the first ring to form a "crown" shape.
- Sprinkle the top with sliced almonds and granulated sugar.
- Bake for 30-35 minutes, or until golden brown and puffed. Turn off the oven and leave the choux pastry in the oven for 10 minutes to dry out. Remove and let cool completely on a wire rack.

2. Prepare the Praline Cream Filling:

- In a large bowl, whip the heavy cream until soft peaks form. Gradually add the powdered sugar and continue to whip until stiff peaks form.
- Gently fold in the praline paste until well combined.

3. Assemble the Paris-Brest:

- Once the choux pastry is completely cool, slice the ring in half horizontally.
- Pipe or spread the praline cream filling evenly over the bottom half of the pastry.
- Place the top half of the pastry on top of the cream filling.

4. Serve:

- Dust with powdered sugar before serving, if desired.

Enjoy your Paris-Brest, a delicious and elegant treat perfect for special occasions or just a delightful indulgence!

Mousse au Chocolat Cake

Ingredients:

For the Chocolate Cake Base:

- 1 cup (125 g) all-purpose flour
- 1 cup (200 g) granulated sugar
- 1/2 cup (50 g) unsweetened cocoa powder
- 1/2 teaspoon baking powder
- 1/2 teaspoon baking soda
- 1/4 teaspoon salt
- 1/2 cup (120 ml) vegetable oil
- 1/2 cup (120 ml) boiling water
- 2 large eggs
- 1/2 cup (120 ml) buttermilk (or 1/2 cup milk with 1 tablespoon lemon juice or vinegar)
- 1 teaspoon vanilla extract

For the Chocolate Mousse:

- 8 oz (225 g) dark chocolate, chopped
- 1 cup (240 ml) heavy cream
- 3 large egg yolks
- 1/2 cup (100 g) granulated sugar
- 1/2 cup (120 ml) milk
- 1 teaspoon vanilla extract
- 1/4 teaspoon salt

For the Ganache Topping (optional):

- 1/2 cup (120 ml) heavy cream
- 4 oz (115 g) dark chocolate, chopped
- 1 tablespoon unsalted butter

Instructions:

1. Prepare the Chocolate Cake Base:

- Preheat your oven to 350°F (175°C). Grease and line the bottom of an 8-inch (20 cm) round cake pan with parchment paper.
- In a large bowl, sift together the flour, sugar, cocoa powder, baking powder, baking soda, and salt.
- In another bowl, whisk together the oil, boiling water, eggs, buttermilk, and vanilla extract.
- Add the wet ingredients to the dry ingredients and mix until just combined.

- Pour the batter into the prepared cake pan and smooth the top.
- Bake for 25-30 minutes, or until a toothpick inserted into the center comes out clean. Let the cake cool in the pan for 10 minutes before transferring it to a wire rack to cool completely.

2. Prepare the Chocolate Mousse:

- Melt the chocolate in a heatproof bowl over a pot of simmering water (double boiler method) or in the microwave in 20-second intervals, stirring until smooth. Let it cool slightly.
- In a small saucepan, heat the milk until just boiling.
- In a bowl, whisk together the egg yolks and granulated sugar until thick and pale. Gradually whisk in the hot milk.
- Return the mixture to the saucepan and cook over medium heat, stirring constantly, until it thickens slightly (170°F or 77°C). Do not let it boil.
- Remove from heat and stir in the melted chocolate, vanilla extract, and salt. Let it cool to room temperature.
- Whip the heavy cream to soft peaks, then fold it gently into the chocolate mixture until fully combined.

3. Assemble the Cake:

- Once the cake is completely cool, cut it in half horizontally to create two layers.
- Place one layer on a serving plate or cake board. Spread or pipe a layer of chocolate mousse evenly over the cake.
- Top with the second cake layer and spread the remaining mousse evenly over the top and sides of the cake.
- Refrigerate the cake for at least 4 hours, or until the mousse is set.

4. Prepare the Ganache Topping (optional):

- In a small saucepan, heat the heavy cream until it begins to simmer.
- Pour the cream over the chopped chocolate in a heatproof bowl. Let it sit for 2 minutes, then stir until smooth.
- Stir in the butter until glossy.
- Allow the ganache to cool slightly before pouring it over the chilled cake.

5. Serve:

- Decorate the cake with chocolate shavings, fresh berries, or a dusting of cocoa powder if desired.
- Slice and serve chilled.

Enjoy your rich and creamy Mousse au Chocolat Cake!

Charlotte aux Fruits

Ingredients:

For the Fruit Filling:

- 3 cups (720 ml) mixed fruit (such as berries, mango, or peaches), chopped if large
- 1/4 cup (50 g) granulated sugar
- 1 tablespoon lemon juice
- 1 tablespoon cornstarch
- 1/2 cup (120 ml) water

For the Bavarois (Cream Filling):

- 1 cup (240 ml) heavy cream
- 1/2 cup (100 g) granulated sugar
- 1 teaspoon vanilla extract
- 2 large egg yolks
- 1/2 cup (120 ml) milk
- 1 tablespoon unflavored gelatin
- 2 tablespoons water (for gelatin)

For the Ladyfingers (Biscuits à la Cuillère):

- 2 large eggs, separated
- 1/2 cup (100 g) granulated sugar
- 1/2 teaspoon vanilla extract
- 1/2 cup (60 g) all-purpose flour
- Powdered sugar, for dusting

Instructions:

1. Prepare the Fruit Filling:

- In a saucepan, combine the mixed fruit, sugar, and lemon juice. Cook over medium heat until the fruit is softened, about 5-7 minutes.
- In a small bowl, dissolve the cornstarch in water. Stir into the fruit mixture and cook until thickened. Let cool.

2. Prepare the Bavarois (Cream Filling):

- In a small bowl, sprinkle the gelatin over 2 tablespoons of water and let it bloom for 5 minutes.
- In a saucepan, heat the milk until it is just about to boil.
- In a bowl, whisk the egg yolks with sugar until thick and pale. Gradually whisk in the hot milk.

- Return the mixture to the saucepan and cook over medium heat, stirring constantly, until it thickens slightly (170°F or 77°C). Do not boil.
- Remove from heat and stir in the bloomed gelatin until completely dissolved. Let cool to room temperature.
- Whip the heavy cream to soft peaks and gently fold it into the cooled custard mixture.

3. Prepare the Ladyfingers:

- Preheat your oven to 350°F (175°C). Line a baking sheet with parchment paper.
- In a bowl, beat the egg whites until soft peaks form. Gradually add the sugar and beat until stiff peaks form.
- Gently fold in the egg yolks and vanilla extract.
- Sift the flour over the mixture and fold gently until combined.
- Pipe or spoon the batter into 4-inch (10 cm) long strips on the prepared baking sheet.
- Dust with powdered sugar and bake for 10-12 minutes, or until golden. Let cool.

4. Assemble the Charlotte:

- Line a 6-inch (15 cm) round cake pan or mold with parchment paper.
- Arrange the ladyfingers around the sides of the pan, trimming them if necessary to fit.
- Spoon half of the fruit filling into the bottom of the pan.
- Spread half of the bavarois over the fruit filling.
- Add the remaining fruit filling and top with the remaining bavarois.
- Chill in the refrigerator for at least 4 hours, or until set.

5. Serve:

- Carefully remove the Charlotte from the pan. Serve chilled, optionally garnished with fresh fruit or a mint sprig.

Enjoy this light and refreshing dessert!

Battenberg Cake (French twist)

Ingredients:

For the Cake:

- 1 cup (125 g) all-purpose flour
- 1 cup (225 g) unsalted butter, softened
- 1 cup (200 g) granulated sugar
- 4 large eggs
- 1 teaspoon vanilla extract
- 1 teaspoon almond extract
- 1 teaspoon baking powder
- 1/4 teaspoon salt
- 1/4 cup (60 ml) milk
- Red and green food coloring (or colors of your choice)

For the Apricot Glaze:

- 1/2 cup (160 g) apricot jam

For the Marzipan:

- 1 1/2 cups (200 g) marzipan (store-bought or homemade)
- Powdered sugar, for rolling out

Instructions:

1. Prepare the Cake:

- Preheat your oven to 350°F (175°C). Grease and line an 8-inch (20 cm) square cake pan with parchment paper.
- In a bowl, cream together the butter and sugar until light and fluffy. Beat in the eggs one at a time, then add the vanilla and almond extracts.
- Sift the flour, baking powder, and salt together. Gradually fold into the butter mixture, alternating with the milk, until just combined.
- Divide the batter evenly into two bowls. Tint one bowl with red food coloring and the other with green food coloring (or other colors as desired).
- Spoon the red batter into one half of the prepared pan and the green batter into the other half, smoothing the top with a spatula.

2. Bake and Assemble:

- Bake for 25-30 minutes, or until a toothpick inserted into the center comes out clean. Allow the cakes to cool in the pan for 10 minutes, then transfer to a wire rack to cool completely.

- Once cooled, trim the edges of each cake and cut each into evenly sized strips.

3. Assemble the Cake:

- Heat the apricot jam in a small saucepan until it becomes liquid. Strain through a sieve to remove any pieces of fruit.
- Brush a thin layer of apricot glaze on a cake board or serving plate. Arrange the alternating colored cake strips in a checkerboard pattern on the board, adhering them together with a layer of apricot glaze.
- Roll out the marzipan on a surface dusted with powdered sugar. It should be large enough to cover the entire cake.
- Brush the top and sides of the assembled cake with more apricot glaze and carefully cover with marzipan, smoothing out any wrinkles. Trim any excess marzipan.

4. Serve:

- Chill the cake to set the marzipan before slicing.

Enjoy your French twist on Battenberg Cake, with its vibrant colors and refined flavors!

Gâteau au Yaourt

Ingredients:

- 1 cup (240 g) plain yogurt (full-fat or low-fat)
- 1 cup (200 g) granulated sugar
- 1/2 cup (120 ml) vegetable oil
- 3 large eggs
- 1 1/2 cups (190 g) all-purpose flour
- 1 1/2 teaspoons baking powder
- 1/4 teaspoon salt
- 1 teaspoon vanilla extract
- Zest of 1 lemon (optional)

Instructions:

1. Preheat Oven:

- Preheat your oven to 350°F (175°C). Grease and flour an 8-inch (20 cm) round cake pan or line it with parchment paper.

2. Mix Ingredients:

- In a large bowl, whisk together the yogurt, sugar, and eggs until smooth.
- Gradually mix in the oil and vanilla extract.
- In another bowl, sift together the flour, baking powder, and salt.
- Fold the dry ingredients into the wet ingredients until just combined. Be careful not to overmix.
- Stir in the lemon zest if using.

3. Bake:

- Pour the batter into the prepared cake pan and smooth the top.
- Bake for 30-35 minutes, or until a toothpick inserted into the center comes out clean.
- Let the cake cool in the pan for 10 minutes before transferring it to a wire rack to cool completely.

4. Serve:

- Dust with powdered sugar or drizzle with a simple glaze if desired.

Enjoy this easy and versatile French yogurt cake, perfect for any occasion!

Mocha Cake

Ingredients:

For the Cake:

- 1 3/4 cups (220 g) all-purpose flour
- 1 1/2 cups (300 g) granulated sugar
- 3/4 cup (65 g) unsweetened cocoa powder
- 1 1/2 teaspoons baking powder
- 1 1/2 teaspoons baking soda
- 1/2 teaspoon salt
- 1 cup (240 ml) hot coffee
- 1/2 cup (120 ml) vegetable oil
- 2 large eggs
- 1 cup (240 ml) buttermilk (or 1 cup milk with 1 tablespoon lemon juice or vinegar)
- 1 teaspoon vanilla extract

For the Mocha Frosting:

- 1 cup (230 g) unsalted butter, softened
- 3 cups (360 g) powdered sugar
- 1/2 cup (45 g) unsweetened cocoa powder
- 2 tablespoons instant coffee granules
- 2 tablespoons hot water
- 2 tablespoons heavy cream (or milk)

Instructions:

1. Prepare the Cake:

- Preheat your oven to 350°F (175°C). Grease and flour two 9-inch (23 cm) round cake pans.
- In a large bowl, whisk together the flour, sugar, cocoa powder, baking powder, baking soda, and salt.
- In another bowl, mix the hot coffee, oil, eggs, buttermilk, and vanilla extract.
- Gradually add the wet ingredients to the dry ingredients, mixing until just combined.
- Divide the batter evenly between the prepared pans and smooth the tops.
- Bake for 30-35 minutes, or until a toothpick inserted into the center comes out clean.
- Let the cakes cool in the pans for 10 minutes before transferring to a wire rack to cool completely.

2. Prepare the Mocha Frosting:

- In a small bowl, dissolve the instant coffee granules in hot water and let cool slightly.

- In a large bowl, beat the butter until creamy. Gradually add the powdered sugar and cocoa powder, beating until smooth.
- Mix in the dissolved coffee and heavy cream until the frosting is light and spreadable. Adjust consistency with more cream if needed.

3. Assemble the Cake:

- If the cakes have domed tops, level them with a knife. Place one cake layer on a serving plate or cake board.
- Spread a layer of mocha frosting on top of the first cake layer.
- Place the second cake layer on top and frost the top and sides of the cake with the remaining mocha frosting.

4. Serve:

- Garnish with chocolate shavings or coffee beans if desired.

Enjoy your indulgent Mocha Cake, perfect for coffee lovers!

Gâteau Saint-Honoré

Ingredients:

For the Pâte à Choux (Choux Pastry):

- 1/2 cup (115 g) unsalted butter
- 1 cup (240 ml) water
- 1/4 teaspoon salt
- 1 cup (125 g) all-purpose flour
- 4 large eggs

For the Pâte Brisée (Shortcrust Pastry):

- 1 1/4 cups (155 g) all-purpose flour
- 1/2 cup (115 g) unsalted butter, cold and cut into cubes
- 1/4 cup (50 g) granulated sugar
- 1 large egg yolk
- 2-3 tablespoons ice water

For the Pastry Cream:

- 2 cups (480 ml) whole milk
- 1/2 cup (100 g) granulated sugar
- 1/4 cup (25 g) cornstarch
- 4 large egg yolks
- 2 tablespoons unsalted butter
- 1 teaspoon vanilla extract

For the Caramel:

- 1 cup (200 g) granulated sugar
- 1/4 cup (60 ml) water

For the Whipped Cream:

- 1 cup (240 ml) heavy cream
- 2 tablespoons powdered sugar

Instructions:

1. Prepare the Pâte Brisée:

- In a bowl or food processor, combine the flour and sugar. Add the cold butter and mix until the mixture resembles coarse crumbs.
- Add the egg yolk and ice water, mixing until the dough comes together.

- Roll out the dough and line the bottom of an 8-inch (20 cm) round cake pan. Prick the bottom with a fork.
- Preheat your oven to 375°F (190°C). Bake the pastry for 15-20 minutes or until golden. Let cool.

2. Prepare the Pâte à Choux:

- In a saucepan, bring the butter, water, and salt to a boil.
- Add the flour all at once and stir vigorously until the mixture forms a smooth ball and pulls away from the sides of the pan.
- Remove from heat and let cool slightly. Beat in the eggs one at a time until the dough is smooth and shiny.
- Pipe small rounds of dough around the edge of the baked pastry shell and bake at 375°F (190°C) for 20-25 minutes, or until golden and puffed. Let cool.

3. Prepare the Pastry Cream:

- In a saucepan, heat the milk until just boiling.
- In a bowl, whisk together the sugar, cornstarch, and egg yolks. Gradually whisk in the hot milk.
- Return the mixture to the saucepan and cook over medium heat, whisking constantly, until thickened and just boiling. Remove from heat and stir in the butter and vanilla extract. Let cool.

4. Prepare the Caramel:

- In a saucepan, combine the sugar and water. Cook over medium heat until the mixture turns a deep amber color. Do not stir.
- Remove from heat and let cool slightly. Dip the tops of the puff pastries in the caramel and let set.

5. Assemble the Cake:

- Spread the pastry cream evenly over the cooled tart shell.
- Arrange the caramel-coated puff pastries around the edge of the tart.
- Whip the cream with powdered sugar until stiff peaks form and pipe or spread over the top of the cake.

6. Serve:

- Chill the cake before serving.

Enjoy your Gâteau Saint-Honoré, a sophisticated and delicious French classic!

Pain d'Épices

Ingredients:

For the Bread:

- 2 cups (250 g) all-purpose flour
- 1/2 cup (100 g) brown sugar
- 1/2 cup (120 ml) honey
- 1 cup (240 ml) milk
- 1/2 cup (120 ml) orange juice
- 1 teaspoon ground cinnamon
- 1/2 teaspoon ground ginger
- 1/2 teaspoon ground cloves
- 1/4 teaspoon ground nutmeg
- 1 teaspoon baking powder
- 1/2 teaspoon baking soda
- 1/2 teaspoon salt

For Optional Add-ins:

- 1/2 cup (75 g) chopped nuts (such as almonds or walnuts)
- 1/2 cup (75 g) dried fruit (such as raisins or apricots)

Instructions:

1. Prepare the Oven and Pan:

- Preheat your oven to 325°F (165°C). Grease and flour a 9x5-inch (23x13 cm) loaf pan, or line it with parchment paper.

2. Mix Dry Ingredients:

- In a large bowl, whisk together the flour, brown sugar, cinnamon, ginger, cloves, nutmeg, baking powder, baking soda, and salt.

3. Combine Wet Ingredients:

- In a separate bowl, mix together the honey, milk, and orange juice until well combined.

4. Combine Wet and Dry Ingredients:

- Pour the wet ingredients into the dry ingredients and stir until just combined. Do not overmix.
- If using, fold in the chopped nuts and dried fruit.

5. Bake the Bread:

- Pour the batter into the prepared loaf pan and smooth the top.
- Bake for 50-60 minutes, or until a toothpick inserted into the center comes out clean.
- Let the bread cool in the pan for 10 minutes, then transfer to a wire rack to cool completely.

6. Serve:

- Pain d'Épices is delicious on its own or served with a bit of butter or jam. It can also be enjoyed with tea or coffee.

Enjoy your Pain d'Épices, a warm and comforting French treat perfect for any time of year!

Baba au Rhum

Ingredients:

For the Baba Dough:

- 1/2 cup (120 ml) whole milk
- 1/4 cup (60 g) unsalted butter
- 1/4 cup (50 g) granulated sugar
- 1 1/2 teaspoons active dry yeast
- 2 large eggs
- 2 cups (250 g) all-purpose flour
- 1/4 teaspoon salt

For the Rum Syrup:

- 1 cup (200 g) granulated sugar
- 1 cup (240 ml) water
- 1/2 cup (120 ml) dark rum
- 1 teaspoon vanilla extract

For the Whipped Cream:

- 1 cup (240 ml) heavy cream
- 2 tablespoons powdered sugar
- 1 teaspoon vanilla extract

Optional Garnish:

- Fresh berries
- Mint leaves

Instructions:

1. Prepare the Baba Dough:

- In a small saucepan, heat the milk until warm but not hot (about 110°F or 45°C). Remove from heat and stir in the butter until melted. Let cool to lukewarm.
- Stir the yeast into the warm milk mixture and let sit for 5 minutes until foamy.
- In a large bowl, whisk together the flour, sugar, and salt. Make a well in the center and pour in the milk mixture and eggs.
- Mix until a smooth dough forms. Knead briefly until the dough is soft and elastic.
- Cover the bowl with plastic wrap and let the dough rise in a warm place for about 1 hour, or until doubled in size.

2. Bake the Baba:

- Preheat your oven to 375°F (190°C). Grease and flour baba molds or a muffin tin (you can also use a bundt pan if you prefer).
- Punch down the risen dough and divide it evenly among the prepared molds, filling each about 2/3 full.
- Bake for 15-20 minutes, or until golden brown and a toothpick inserted into the center comes out clean.
- Remove from the oven and let cool in the molds for 5 minutes before transferring to a wire rack.

3. Prepare the Rum Syrup:

- In a saucepan, combine the sugar and water. Heat over medium heat, stirring occasionally, until the sugar is completely dissolved.
- Remove from heat and stir in the rum and vanilla extract. Let cool slightly.

4. Soak the Babas:

- Once the babas are slightly cooled but still warm, place them in a shallow dish and pour the rum syrup over them. Allow the babas to soak in the syrup for about 15-20 minutes, turning occasionally, until fully absorbed.

5. Prepare the Whipped Cream:

- In a mixing bowl, whip the heavy cream with powdered sugar and vanilla extract until soft peaks form.

6. Serve:

- Place the soaked babas on serving plates. Top with a dollop of whipped cream and garnish with fresh berries and mint leaves, if desired.

Enjoy your Baba au Rhum, a delightful and indulgent French classic!

Gâteau de Crêpes

Ingredients:

For the Crêpes:

- 1 cup (125 g) all-purpose flour
- 2 large eggs
- 1 1/4 cups (300 ml) milk
- 2 tablespoons melted butter
- 1/4 teaspoon salt
- 1 tablespoon granulated sugar (optional)

For the Filling:

- 2 cups (480 ml) heavy cream
- 1/4 cup (50 g) granulated sugar
- 1 teaspoon vanilla extract
- 1 cup (250 g) ricotta cheese or mascarpone cheese
- 1/2 cup (120 ml) fruit compote or jam (such as raspberry, apricot, or strawberry)

Instructions:

1. Prepare the Crêpes:

- In a large bowl, whisk together the flour, eggs, milk, melted butter, salt, and sugar (if using) until smooth. Let the batter rest for at least 30 minutes.
- Heat a non-stick skillet or crêpe pan over medium heat and lightly grease it with butter or oil.
- Pour a small amount of batter into the pan and swirl to coat the bottom evenly. Cook for about 1-2 minutes until the edges start to lift and the bottom is lightly golden. Flip and cook for another 30 seconds to 1 minute. Repeat with the remaining batter, stacking the cooked crêpes on a plate.

2. Prepare the Filling:

- In a mixing bowl, whip the heavy cream with the granulated sugar and vanilla extract until soft peaks form.
- Gently fold in the ricotta or mascarpone cheese until well combined.

3. Assemble the Gâteau de Crêpes:

- Place one crêpe on a serving plate or cake stand. Spread a thin layer of the filling over the crêpe.
- Top with another crêpe and repeat the process until all crêpes and filling are used, ending with a crêpe on top.

- Spread a thin layer of fruit compote or jam over the top crêpe.

4. Chill and Serve:

- Refrigerate the cake for at least 1 hour to allow the flavors to meld and the filling to set.
- Slice and serve chilled or at room temperature. Garnish with fresh berries or a dusting of powdered sugar if desired.

Enjoy your Gâteau de Crêpes, a versatile and charming French dessert perfect for any occasion!

Tarte aux Pommes

Ingredients:

For the Pastry:

- 1 1/4 cups (160 g) all-purpose flour
- 1/2 cup (115 g) unsalted butter, cold and cut into cubes
- 1/4 cup (50 g) granulated sugar
- 1/4 teaspoon salt
- 1 large egg yolk
- 2-3 tablespoons ice water

For the Apple Filling:

- 4-5 medium apples (such as Granny Smith or Honeycrisp), peeled, cored, and thinly sliced
- 1/4 cup (50 g) granulated sugar
- 1/4 teaspoon ground cinnamon
- 1 tablespoon lemon juice
- 2 tablespoons unsalted butter, melted
- 1 tablespoon all-purpose flour

For the Glaze (optional):

- 1/4 cup (60 ml) apricot jam or jelly
- 1 tablespoon water

Instructions:

1. Prepare the Pastry:

- In a large bowl or food processor, combine the flour, sugar, and salt. Add the cold butter and mix until the mixture resembles coarse crumbs.
- Stir in the egg yolk. Add ice water, one tablespoon at a time, until the dough just comes together. Do not overmix.
- Form the dough into a disk, wrap in plastic wrap, and chill in the refrigerator for at least 30 minutes.

2. Prepare the Apple Filling:

- Preheat your oven to 375°F (190°C).
- In a large bowl, toss the apple slices with sugar, cinnamon, and lemon juice. Set aside.

3. Roll Out the Pastry:

- On a lightly floured surface, roll out the chilled pastry dough to fit a 9-inch (23 cm) tart pan. Gently press the dough into the pan and trim the edges.
- Place the tart shell in the freezer for 10 minutes.

4. Bake the Tart Shell:

- Line the tart shell with parchment paper and fill with pie weights or dried beans. Bake for 10 minutes.
- Remove the parchment and weights and bake for an additional 5 minutes, or until the shell is lightly golden. Let cool.

5. Assemble the Tart:

- Arrange the apple slices in concentric circles over the baked tart shell. Brush with melted butter and sprinkle with flour.
- Bake for 30-35 minutes, or until the apples are tender and the crust is golden brown.

6. Prepare the Glaze (optional):

- In a small saucepan, heat the apricot jam and water over low heat until melted and smooth.
- Brush the glaze over the apples while the tart is still warm.

7. Serve:

- Let the tart cool before slicing. Serve plain or with a dollop of crème fraîche or vanilla ice cream if desired.

Enjoy your **Tarte aux Pommes**, a delightful and classic French dessert perfect for any occasion!

Canelés

Ingredients:

For the Batter:

- 2 cups (500 ml) whole milk
- 1 tablespoon unsalted butter
- 1 vanilla bean or 1 tablespoon vanilla extract
- 2 large eggs
- 1 egg yolk
- 1 cup (200 g) granulated sugar
- 1 cup (125 g) all-purpose flour
- 2 tablespoons dark rum

For the Molds:

- 2 tablespoons unsalted butter (for greasing)
- 1/4 cup (50 g) granulated sugar (for dusting)

Instructions:

1. Prepare the Batter:

- In a saucepan, heat the milk and butter until the butter is melted and the milk is warm. If using a vanilla bean, split it, scrape out the seeds, and add both seeds and pod to the milk. Otherwise, add vanilla extract once removed from heat.
- Let the mixture cool slightly, then remove the vanilla bean pod if used.
- In a bowl, whisk together the eggs, egg yolk, and sugar until pale and fluffy. Gradually add the flour, mixing until smooth.
- Stir in the warm milk mixture and the rum until well combined. The batter should be thin and well blended.
- Cover the bowl and refrigerate for at least 24 hours (up to 48 hours) to let the flavors meld.

2. Prepare the Molds:

- Preheat your oven to 425°F (220°C).
- Generously butter the canelé molds and dust them with granulated sugar, tapping out any excess.

3. Bake the Canelés:

- Pour the chilled batter into the prepared molds, filling them almost to the top.

- Bake for 15 minutes at 425°F (220°C), then reduce the temperature to 375°F (190°C) and bake for an additional 40-45 minutes, or until the canelés are deeply caramelized and have a crispy, dark exterior.
- The canelés should come away from the molds easily when inverted. Let them cool on a wire rack.

4. Serve:

- Canelés are best enjoyed fresh but can be kept in an airtight container for a few days. Reheat in a 350°F (175°C) oven for a few minutes to regain crispness if needed.

Enjoy your deliciously crisp and custardy **Canelés**, a true French treat!

Quatre-Quarts

Ingredients:

- 1 cup (225 g) unsalted butter, softened
- 1 cup (200 g) granulated sugar
- 4 large eggs
- 1 cup (125 g) all-purpose flour
- 1 cup (125 g) almond flour (or you can use additional all-purpose flour)
- 1 teaspoon baking powder
- 1/4 teaspoon salt
- 1 teaspoon vanilla extract
- Zest of 1 lemon (optional)

Instructions:

1. Preheat Oven:

- Preheat your oven to 350°F (175°C). Grease and flour a 9x5-inch (23x13 cm) loaf pan or line it with parchment paper.

2. Prepare the Batter:

- In a large bowl, cream together the softened butter and sugar until light and fluffy.
- Beat in the eggs one at a time, making sure each is fully incorporated before adding the next.
- Mix in the vanilla extract and lemon zest, if using.
- In a separate bowl, whisk together the all-purpose flour, almond flour, baking powder, and salt.
- Gradually fold the dry ingredients into the wet ingredients until just combined. Be careful not to overmix.

3. Bake:

- Pour the batter into the prepared loaf pan and smooth the top.
- Bake for 50-60 minutes, or until a toothpick inserted into the center comes out clean and the cake is golden brown.

4. Cool and Serve:

- Let the cake cool in the pan for 10 minutes, then transfer to a wire rack to cool completely.
- Slice and serve plain, or with a dusting of powdered sugar or a glaze if desired.

Enjoy your **Quatre-Quarts**, a delightful and versatile French pound cake that's perfect with a cup of tea or coffee!

Tarte aux Fruits Rouges

Ingredients:

For the Tart Crust:

- 1 1/4 cups (160 g) all-purpose flour
- 1/2 cup (115 g) unsalted butter, cold and cut into cubes
- 1/4 cup (50 g) granulated sugar
- 1/4 teaspoon salt
- 1 large egg yolk
- 1-2 tablespoons ice water

For the Pastry Cream:

- 2 cups (480 ml) whole milk
- 1/2 cup (100 g) granulated sugar
- 1/4 cup (25 g) cornstarch
- 4 large egg yolks
- 2 tablespoons unsalted butter
- 1 teaspoon vanilla extract

For the Topping:

- 2 cups mixed red berries (such as strawberries, raspberries, and blueberries)
- 1/4 cup (60 ml) apricot jam (for glazing)

Instructions:

1. Prepare the Tart Crust:

- In a bowl or food processor, combine the flour, sugar, and salt. Add the cold butter and mix until the mixture resembles coarse crumbs.
- Stir in the egg yolk. Add ice water, one tablespoon at a time, until the dough just comes together.
- Shape the dough into a disk, wrap in plastic wrap, and refrigerate for at least 30 minutes.

2. Preheat Oven and Bake the Crust:

- Preheat your oven to 375°F (190°C).
- Roll out the chilled dough on a lightly floured surface and fit it into a 9-inch (23 cm) tart pan. Trim any excess dough.
- Line the tart shell with parchment paper and fill with pie weights or dried beans. Bake for 15 minutes.
- Remove the parchment and weights, and bake for an additional 5-7 minutes until the crust is golden brown. Let cool.

3. Prepare the Pastry Cream:

- In a saucepan, heat the milk until just boiling. In a bowl, whisk together the sugar, cornstarch, and egg yolks.
- Gradually whisk the hot milk into the egg mixture, then return the mixture to the saucepan.
- Cook over medium heat, whisking constantly, until thickened and boiling. Remove from heat and stir in the butter and vanilla extract. Let cool.

4. Assemble the Tart:

- Spread the cooled pastry cream evenly over the baked tart shell.
- Arrange the mixed berries on top of the pastry cream.

5. Glaze the Tart:

- In a small saucepan, gently heat the apricot jam until it becomes liquid. Brush the warm jam over the berries to give them a glossy finish.

6. Serve:

- Chill the tart in the refrigerator for at least 1 hour before serving.

Enjoy your **Tarte aux Fruits Rouges**, a refreshing and beautiful dessert perfect for showcasing seasonal berries!

Tarte Bourdaloue

Ingredients:

For the Tart Crust:

- 1 1/4 cups (160 g) all-purpose flour
- 1/2 cup (115 g) unsalted butter, cold and cut into cubes
- 1/4 cup (50 g) granulated sugar
- 1/4 teaspoon salt
- 1 large egg yolk
- 1-2 tablespoons ice water

For the Almond Cream (Frangipane):

- 1/2 cup (115 g) unsalted butter, softened
- 1/2 cup (100 g) granulated sugar
- 1 cup (100 g) almond flour
- 2 large eggs
- 1 teaspoon vanilla extract
- 1 tablespoon all-purpose flour

For the Poached Pears:

- 2 ripe pears, peeled, cored, and halved
- 1 cup (240 ml) water
- 1/2 cup (100 g) granulated sugar
- 1 teaspoon vanilla extract
- 1 cinnamon stick

For the Glaze (optional):

- 1/4 cup (60 ml) apricot jam
- 1 tablespoon water

Instructions:

1. Prepare the Tart Crust:

- In a bowl or food processor, combine the flour, sugar, and salt. Add the cold butter and mix until the mixture resembles coarse crumbs.
- Stir in the egg yolk and mix until the dough just comes together. Add ice water if needed.
- Shape the dough into a disk, wrap in plastic wrap, and refrigerate for at least 30 minutes.

2. Prepare the Almond Cream:

- In a mixing bowl, beat the softened butter and sugar together until light and fluffy.
- Mix in the almond flour, eggs, vanilla extract, and flour until smooth.

3. Poach the Pears:

- In a saucepan, combine water, sugar, vanilla extract, and cinnamon stick. Bring to a simmer.
- Add the pear halves and simmer for about 10-15 minutes until tender but still holding their shape. Remove the pears from the liquid and let cool.

4. Preheat Oven and Bake the Crust:

- Preheat your oven to 375°F (190°C).
- Roll out the chilled dough on a lightly floured surface and fit it into a 9-inch (23 cm) tart pan. Trim any excess dough.
- Line the tart shell with parchment paper and fill with pie weights or dried beans. Bake for 15 minutes.
- Remove the parchment and weights, and bake for an additional 5-7 minutes until golden brown. Let cool.

5. Assemble the Tart:

- Spread the almond cream evenly over the baked tart shell.
- Arrange the poached pear halves on top of the almond cream.
- Bake for 30-35 minutes, or until the almond cream is set and golden brown.

6. Glaze the Tart (optional):

- In a small saucepan, heat the apricot jam and water until melted and smooth.
- Brush the glaze over the pears to give them a shiny finish.

7. Serve:

- Let the tart cool before serving. It's delicious on its own or served with a dollop of whipped cream or a scoop of vanilla ice cream.

Enjoy your **Tarte Bourdaloue**, a refined and delectable French pastry that's sure to impress!

Bûche de Noël

Ingredients:

For the Sponge Cake:

- 4 large eggs
- 1 cup (200 g) granulated sugar
- 1/2 cup (60 g) all-purpose flour
- 1/2 cup (60 g) cocoa powder
- 1/4 teaspoon baking powder
- 1/4 teaspoon salt
- 1 teaspoon vanilla extract

For the Chocolate Ganache Filling and Frosting:

- 1 cup (240 ml) heavy cream
- 8 oz (225 g) semisweet chocolate, chopped
- 2 tablespoons unsalted butter

For the Decorations:

- Powdered sugar (for dusting)
- Fresh berries or holly leaves (optional)

Instructions:

1. Prepare the Sponge Cake:

- Preheat your oven to 375°F (190°C). Line a 15x10-inch (38x25 cm) jelly roll pan with parchment paper.
- In a large bowl, beat the eggs and sugar together until thick and pale.
- Sift together the flour, cocoa powder, baking powder, and salt. Gently fold into the egg mixture, along with the vanilla extract.
- Pour the batter into the prepared pan and spread evenly.
- Bake for 10-12 minutes, or until the cake is springy to the touch and a toothpick inserted into the center comes out clean.
- While the cake is still warm, turn it out onto a clean kitchen towel dusted with powdered sugar. Peel off the parchment paper and roll the cake up with the towel, starting from the short end. Let cool.

2. Prepare the Chocolate Ganache:

- In a saucepan, heat the heavy cream until just boiling.
- Pour the hot cream over the chopped chocolate in a heatproof bowl. Let sit for a few minutes, then stir until smooth.

- Stir in the butter until the ganache is glossy and smooth. Let cool to room temperature before using.

3. Assemble the Bûche de Noël:

- Unroll the cooled cake and spread a thin layer of ganache over the surface.
- Roll the cake back up carefully without the towel, and place it seam-side down on a serving platter.
- Frost the outside of the cake with the remaining ganache, smoothing it out with a spatula. Use a fork to create a bark-like texture.
- Chill the cake in the refrigerator for at least an hour to set the ganache.

4. Decorate:

- Dust the cake with powdered sugar to resemble snow. Decorate with fresh berries, holly leaves, or other festive touches if desired.

5. Serve:

- Slice and serve chilled or at room temperature. Enjoy your festive **Bûche de Noël**, a classic and charming holiday treat!

Marquise au Chocolat

Ingredients:

- 8 oz (225 g) bittersweet or semisweet chocolate, chopped
- 4 large eggs, separated
- 1/2 cup (100 g) granulated sugar
- 1 cup (240 ml) heavy cream
- 1 teaspoon vanilla extract
- Pinch of salt

Instructions:

1. Melt the Chocolate:

- In a heatproof bowl, melt the chocolate over a pot of simmering water (double boiler method), stirring until smooth. Let it cool slightly.

2. Prepare the Egg Yolks:

- In a bowl, whisk the egg yolks and half of the sugar until pale and slightly thickened.
- Gently fold the melted chocolate into the egg yolk mixture until well combined.

3. Whip the Egg Whites:

- In a clean bowl, beat the egg whites with a pinch of salt until soft peaks form. Gradually add the remaining sugar and continue beating until stiff peaks form.
- Gently fold the beaten egg whites into the chocolate mixture in three parts, being careful not to deflate the mixture.

4. Whip the Cream:

- In a separate bowl, whip the heavy cream and vanilla extract until soft peaks form.
- Fold the whipped cream into the chocolate mixture until well combined.

5. Chill:

- Spoon the mixture into individual serving dishes or one large serving dish.
- Refrigerate for at least 4 hours, or until set.

6. Serve:

- Garnish with shaved chocolate, fresh berries, or a dollop of whipped cream if desired.

Enjoy your **Marquise au Chocolat**, a luxurious and indulgent chocolate treat!

Tarte au Chocolat

Ingredients:

For the Tart Crust:

- 1 1/4 cups (160 g) all-purpose flour
- 1/2 cup (115 g) unsalted butter, cold and cut into cubes
- 1/4 cup (50 g) granulated sugar
- 1/4 teaspoon salt
- 1 large egg yolk
- 1-2 tablespoons ice water

For the Chocolate Filling:

- 8 oz (225 g) bittersweet or semisweet chocolate, chopped
- 1 cup (240 ml) heavy cream
- 2 large eggs
- 1 teaspoon vanilla extract
- 1/4 cup (50 g) granulated sugar (optional, depending on the sweetness of your chocolate)

For Garnish (optional):

- Whipped cream
- Fresh berries
- Chocolate shavings or curls

Instructions:

1. Prepare the Tart Crust:

- In a bowl or food processor, combine the flour, sugar, and salt. Add the cold butter and mix until the mixture resembles coarse crumbs.
- Stir in the egg yolk and mix until the dough just comes together. Add ice water if needed.
- Shape the dough into a disk, wrap in plastic wrap, and refrigerate for at least 30 minutes.

2. Preheat Oven and Bake the Crust:

- Preheat your oven to 375°F (190°C).
- Roll out the chilled dough on a lightly floured surface and fit it into a 9-inch (23 cm) tart pan. Trim any excess dough.
- Line the tart shell with parchment paper and fill with pie weights or dried beans. Bake for 15 minutes.
- Remove the parchment and weights, and bake for an additional 5-7 minutes until golden brown. Let cool.

3. Prepare the Chocolate Filling:

- In a saucepan, heat the heavy cream until it just begins to simmer. Remove from heat.
- Add the chopped chocolate to the hot cream and let sit for 2-3 minutes to soften. Stir until smooth.
- In a bowl, whisk the eggs and sugar (if using) until well combined. Gradually mix in the chocolate mixture.
- Stir in the vanilla extract.

4. Assemble and Bake:

- Pour the chocolate filling into the baked tart shell.
- Bake at 350°F (175°C) for 15-20 minutes, or until the filling is set but still slightly wobbly in the center.

5. Cool and Garnish:

- Let the tart cool to room temperature, then chill in the refrigerator for at least 2 hours to fully set.
- Garnish with whipped cream, fresh berries, or chocolate shavings before serving if desired.

Enjoy your **Tarte au Chocolat**, a rich and elegant dessert that's sure to impress!

Mille-Feuille

Ingredients:

For the Puff Pastry:

- 1 package (about 14 oz or 400 g) frozen puff pastry, thawed (or homemade if preferred)

For the Pastry Cream:

- 2 cups (480 ml) whole milk
- 1/2 cup (100 g) granulated sugar
- 1/4 cup (25 g) cornstarch
- 4 large egg yolks
- 2 tablespoons unsalted butter
- 1 teaspoon vanilla extract

For the Icing (optional):

- 1 cup (125 g) powdered sugar
- 2-3 tablespoons milk or water
- 1 tablespoon unsweetened cocoa powder (for a chocolate version) or a few drops of vanilla extract

Instructions:

1. Prepare the Puff Pastry:

- Preheat your oven to 400°F (200°C).
- Roll out the puff pastry on a lightly floured surface to about 1/8-inch (3 mm) thickness.
- Cut the pastry into rectangles, typically 3x6-inch (8x15 cm), for a traditional shape.
- Place the rectangles on a baking sheet lined with parchment paper. Prick the pastry all over with a fork to prevent excessive puffing.
- Bake for 15-20 minutes, or until golden and crisp. Let cool completely.

2. Prepare the Pastry Cream:

- In a saucepan, heat the milk until just boiling.
- In a bowl, whisk together the sugar, cornstarch, and egg yolks until smooth.
- Gradually pour the hot milk into the egg mixture, whisking constantly. Return the mixture to the saucepan.
- Cook over medium heat, whisking constantly, until thickened and boiling. Remove from heat and stir in the butter and vanilla extract.
- Transfer to a bowl, cover with plastic wrap (pressing it directly onto the surface of the cream to prevent a skin from forming), and let cool.

3. Assemble the Mille-Feuille:

- Spread a layer of pastry cream over one rectangle of puff pastry. Top with another pastry rectangle and spread more cream on top. Repeat with the remaining layers.
- For a traditional finish, place the final layer of pastry on top and smooth with a spatula.

4. Prepare the Icing (optional):

- Mix powdered sugar with milk or water until smooth to create a simple icing. For a chocolate version, add cocoa powder.
- Spread the icing over the top layer of pastry. Use a fork or toothpick to create a decorative pattern if desired.

5. Chill and Serve:

- Refrigerate the assembled Mille-Feuille for at least an hour before slicing to allow the pastry cream to set and the layers to meld.
- Slice with a serrated knife and serve chilled.

Enjoy your **Mille-Feuille**, a sophisticated and delicious French pastry that's perfect for special occasions!

Tarte aux Abricots

Ingredients:

For the Tart Crust:

- 1 1/4 cups (160 g) all-purpose flour
- 1/2 cup (115 g) unsalted butter, cold and cut into cubes
- 1/4 cup (50 g) granulated sugar
- 1/4 teaspoon salt
- 1 large egg yolk
- 1-2 tablespoons ice water

For the Almond Cream (Frangipane):

- 1/2 cup (115 g) unsalted butter, softened
- 1/2 cup (100 g) granulated sugar
- 1 cup (100 g) almond flour
- 2 large eggs
- 1 teaspoon vanilla extract
- 1 tablespoon all-purpose flour

For the Apricot Topping:

- 4-6 fresh apricots, halved and pitted
- 1/4 cup (50 g) granulated sugar (optional, depending on sweetness of apricots)
- 2 tablespoons apricot jam (for glazing, optional)

Instructions:

1. Prepare the Tart Crust:

- In a bowl or food processor, combine the flour, sugar, and salt. Add the cold butter and mix until the mixture resembles coarse crumbs.
- Stir in the egg yolk and mix until the dough just comes together. Add ice water if needed.
- Shape the dough into a disk, wrap in plastic wrap, and refrigerate for at least 30 minutes.

2. Preheat Oven and Bake the Crust:

- Preheat your oven to 375°F (190°C).
- Roll out the chilled dough on a lightly floured surface and fit it into a 9-inch (23 cm) tart pan. Trim any excess dough.
- Line the tart shell with parchment paper and fill with pie weights or dried beans. Bake for 15 minutes.
- Remove the parchment and weights, and bake for an additional 5-7 minutes until golden brown. Let cool.

3. Prepare the Almond Cream:

- In a bowl, cream the softened butter and sugar together until light and fluffy.
- Mix in the almond flour, eggs, vanilla extract, and flour until smooth.

4. Assemble the Tart:

- Spread the almond cream evenly over the baked tart shell.
- Arrange the apricot halves on top of the almond cream, cut side up. Sprinkle with sugar if desired.

5. Bake:

- Bake at 375°F (190°C) for 30-35 minutes, or until the almond cream is set and golden brown.

6. Glaze the Tart (optional):

- In a small saucepan, gently heat the apricot jam until melted and smooth. Brush over the apricots for a glossy finish.

7. Serve:

- Let the tart cool before slicing. Enjoy it on its own or with a dollop of crème fraîche or vanilla ice cream.

Enjoy your **Tarte aux Abricots**, a beautifully sweet and elegant French treat!

Tartelette au Citron

Ingredients:

For the Tart Shells:

- 1 1/4 cups (160 g) all-purpose flour
- 1/2 cup (115 g) unsalted butter, cold and cut into cubes
- 1/4 cup (50 g) granulated sugar
- 1/4 teaspoon salt
- 1 large egg yolk
- 1-2 tablespoons ice water

For the Lemon Curd:

- 1/2 cup (120 ml) fresh lemon juice (about 3 lemons)
- 1 tablespoon lemon zest (from about 2 lemons)
- 1/2 cup (100 g) granulated sugar
- 3 large eggs
- 1/4 cup (60 g) unsalted butter, cubed

For Garnish (optional):

- Whipped cream
- Lemon zest or thin lemon slices

Instructions:

1. Prepare the Tart Shells:

- In a bowl or food processor, combine the flour, sugar, and salt. Add the cold butter and mix until the mixture resembles coarse crumbs.
- Stir in the egg yolk and mix until the dough just comes together. Add ice water if needed.
- Shape the dough into a disk, wrap in plastic wrap, and refrigerate for at least 30 minutes.

2. Preheat Oven and Bake the Shells:

- Preheat your oven to 375°F (190°C).
- Roll out the chilled dough on a lightly floured surface. Cut out circles to fit into a 12-cup tartlet pan or mini tart pans.
- Press the dough into the pans and trim any excess. Prick the bottoms with a fork.
- Line each tart shell with parchment paper and fill with pie weights or dried beans. Bake for 12-15 minutes.
- Remove the parchment and weights, and bake for an additional 5 minutes until golden brown. Let cool completely.

3. Prepare the Lemon Curd:

- In a heatproof bowl, whisk together the lemon juice, lemon zest, sugar, and eggs.
- Place the bowl over a pot of simmering water (double boiler) and cook, whisking constantly, until the mixture thickens and coats the back of a spoon (about 10-12 minutes). Do not let it boil.
- Remove from heat and stir in the butter until smooth.
- Strain the curd through a fine-mesh sieve into a clean bowl to remove any lumps. Let cool to room temperature.

4. Assemble the Tartlets:

- Spoon or pipe the cooled lemon curd into the baked tart shells.

5. Garnish and Serve:

- Top with a dollop of whipped cream and garnish with additional lemon zest or thin lemon slices if desired.
- Serve chilled or at room temperature.

Enjoy your **Tartelette au Citron**, a refreshing and elegant treat that's perfect for any occasion!

Gâteau aux Noix

Ingredients:

For the Cake:

- 1 cup (120 g) walnut halves (plus extra for decoration)
- 1 cup (200 g) granulated sugar
- 1/2 cup (115 g) unsalted butter, softened
- 3 large eggs
- 1 cup (120 g) all-purpose flour
- 1 teaspoon baking powder
- 1/4 teaspoon salt
- 1 teaspoon vanilla extract
- 1/4 cup (60 ml) milk

For the Glaze (optional):

- 1/2 cup (60 g) powdered sugar
- 2-3 tablespoons milk or water
- 1/4 teaspoon vanilla extract

Instructions:

1. Preheat Oven and Prepare the Pan:

- Preheat your oven to 350°F (175°C).
- Grease and flour an 8-inch (20 cm) round cake pan or line it with parchment paper.

2. Prepare the Walnuts:

- Place the walnuts in a food processor and pulse until finely chopped. You want some texture, so don't over-process into a paste.

3. Make the Cake Batter:

- In a mixing bowl, cream together the softened butter and granulated sugar until light and fluffy.
- Beat in the eggs one at a time, ensuring each is fully incorporated before adding the next.
- Mix in the vanilla extract.
- In a separate bowl, whisk together the flour, baking powder, and salt.
- Gradually add the dry ingredients to the butter mixture, alternating with the milk, beginning and ending with the dry ingredients. Mix until just combined.
- Fold in the chopped walnuts.

4. Bake the Cake:

- Pour the batter into the prepared cake pan and smooth the top.
- Bake for 25-30 minutes, or until a toothpick inserted into the center comes out clean and the cake is golden brown.

5. Cool and Glaze (optional):

- Let the cake cool in the pan for 10 minutes, then transfer to a wire rack to cool completely.
- If desired, make the glaze by mixing powdered sugar with milk or water until smooth. Drizzle over the cooled cake and garnish with additional walnut halves.

6. Serve:

- Slice and enjoy your **Gâteau aux Noix** with a cup of tea or coffee.

This cake is rich with the flavor of walnuts and has a delightful texture. It's perfect for a special occasion or just as a treat to enjoy with family and friends!

Crêpes Suzette Cake

Ingredients:

For the Crêpes:

- 1 cup (125 g) all-purpose flour
- 2 large eggs
- 1 cup (240 ml) milk
- 2 tablespoons granulated sugar
- 1/4 cup (60 g) unsalted butter, melted
- 1/4 teaspoon salt
- 1 teaspoon vanilla extract (optional)

For the Orange Sauce:

- 1/2 cup (120 ml) freshly squeezed orange juice
- 1/4 cup (50 g) granulated sugar
- 2 tablespoons unsalted butter
- 2 tablespoons orange liqueur (like Grand Marnier) or orange extract

For the Filling:

- 1 cup (240 ml) heavy cream
- 2 tablespoons granulated sugar
- 1 teaspoon vanilla extract

For Garnish (optional):

- Orange zest
- Fresh mint leaves

Instructions:

1. Make the Crêpes:

- In a bowl, whisk together the flour, eggs, milk, sugar, melted butter, salt, and vanilla extract until smooth. Let the batter rest for at least 30 minutes.
- Heat a non-stick skillet over medium heat and lightly grease with butter or oil.
- Pour a small amount of batter into the skillet and swirl to cover the bottom evenly. Cook until the edges start to lift, then flip and cook for another 1-2 minutes. Repeat with the remaining batter, stacking the cooked crêpes on a plate. Let cool.

2. Prepare the Orange Sauce:

- In a saucepan, combine the orange juice and sugar. Heat over medium heat until the sugar dissolves and the mixture begins to simmer.
- Add the butter and stir until melted. Remove from heat and stir in the orange liqueur or extract. Let cool slightly.

3. Prepare the Filling:

- In a mixing bowl, whip the heavy cream, sugar, and vanilla extract until soft peaks form.

4. Assemble the Cake:

- Place one crêpe on a serving plate. Spread a thin layer of whipped cream over it.
- Top with another crêpe and continue layering with cream, finishing with a crêpe on top.
- Pour the orange sauce over the top layer of crêpes, allowing it to drizzle down the sides.

5. Garnish and Serve:

- Garnish with orange zest and fresh mint leaves if desired.
- Serve immediately or refrigerate for up to a few hours before serving.

Enjoy your **Crêpes Suzette Cake**, a sophisticated and delicious dessert that beautifully captures the flavors of the classic French dish!

Parisienne Cake

Ingredients:

For the Cake:

- 1 cup (120 g) all-purpose flour
- 1/2 cup (115 g) unsalted butter, softened
- 1 cup (200 g) granulated sugar
- 3 large eggs
- 1 teaspoon vanilla extract
- 1/2 cup (120 ml) milk
- 1 1/2 teaspoons baking powder
- 1/4 teaspoon salt

For the Syrup:

- 1/2 cup (120 ml) water
- 1/2 cup (100 g) granulated sugar
- 2 tablespoons orange liqueur (like Grand Marnier) or orange juice

For the Filling:

- 1 cup (240 ml) heavy cream
- 2 tablespoons granulated sugar
- 1 teaspoon vanilla extract
- Fresh fruit or fruit preserves (like apricot or raspberry) for layering

For the Garnish (optional):

- Fresh berries
- Mint leaves
- Powdered sugar

Instructions:

1. Preheat Oven and Prepare the Pan:

- Preheat your oven to 350°F (175°C).
- Grease and flour an 8-inch (20 cm) round cake pan or line it with parchment paper.

2. Make the Cake:

- In a bowl, cream together the softened butter and sugar until light and fluffy.
- Beat in the eggs one at a time, ensuring each is fully incorporated before adding the next. Mix in the vanilla extract.

- In another bowl, whisk together the flour, baking powder, and salt.
- Gradually add the dry ingredients to the butter mixture, alternating with the milk, beginning and ending with the dry ingredients. Mix until just combined.
- Pour the batter into the prepared cake pan and smooth the top.
- Bake for 25-30 minutes, or until a toothpick inserted into the center comes out clean. Let cool in the pan for 10 minutes, then transfer to a wire rack to cool completely.

3. Prepare the Syrup:

- In a small saucepan, combine water and sugar. Heat until the sugar dissolves and the syrup is clear.
- Remove from heat and stir in the orange liqueur or orange juice. Let cool.

4. Prepare the Filling:

- In a mixing bowl, whip the heavy cream, sugar, and vanilla extract until soft peaks form.

5. Assemble the Cake:

- Slice the cooled cake horizontally into two or three layers.
- Brush each layer with the orange syrup.
- Spread a layer of whipped cream and a layer of fruit preserves or fresh fruit on each layer.
- Stack the layers, finishing with the top layer.

6. Garnish and Serve:

- Garnish with fresh berries, mint leaves, and a dusting of powdered sugar if desired.
- Serve chilled or at room temperature.

Enjoy your **Parisienne Cake**, a sophisticated and flavorful dessert that's perfect for any special occasion!

Tarte au Praliné

Ingredients:

For the Tart Crust:

- 1 1/4 cups (160 g) all-purpose flour
- 1/2 cup (115 g) unsalted butter, cold and cut into cubes
- 1/4 cup (50 g) granulated sugar
- 1/4 teaspoon salt
- 1 large egg yolk
- 1-2 tablespoons ice water

For the Praliné Filling:

- 1 cup (100 g) praliné paste (store-bought or homemade, see note below)
- 1/2 cup (115 g) unsalted butter, softened
- 1/2 cup (100 g) granulated sugar
- 2 large eggs
- 1/2 cup (120 ml) heavy cream
- 1 teaspoon vanilla extract

For Garnish (optional):

- Crushed praline or chopped nuts
- Whipped cream

Instructions:

1. Prepare the Tart Crust:

- In a bowl or food processor, combine the flour, sugar, and salt. Add the cold butter and mix until the mixture resembles coarse crumbs.
- Stir in the egg yolk and mix until the dough just comes together. Add ice water if needed.
- Shape the dough into a disk, wrap in plastic wrap, and refrigerate for at least 30 minutes.

2. Preheat Oven and Bake the Crust:

- Preheat your oven to 375°F (190°C).
- Roll out the chilled dough on a lightly floured surface and fit it into a 9-inch (23 cm) tart pan. Trim any excess dough.
- Line the tart shell with parchment paper and fill with pie weights or dried beans. Bake for 15 minutes.
- Remove the parchment and weights, and bake for an additional 5-7 minutes until golden brown. Let cool completely.

3. Prepare the Praliné Filling:

- In a mixing bowl, beat together the praliné paste, softened butter, and sugar until light and creamy.
- Beat in the eggs one at a time, making sure each is fully incorporated before adding the next.
- Mix in the heavy cream and vanilla extract until smooth.

4. Assemble the Tart:

- Pour the praliné filling into the baked tart shell.
- Bake at 350°F (175°C) for 20-25 minutes, or until the filling is set and lightly browned.

5. Cool and Garnish:

- Let the tart cool completely before removing from the pan.
- Garnish with crushed praline or chopped nuts and a dollop of whipped cream if desired.

6. Serve:

- Slice and serve the tart at room temperature or chilled.

Note:

Homemade Praliné Paste: To make praliné paste at home, you can caramelize nuts (usually almonds or hazelnuts) with sugar and then blend until smooth. Here's a quick overview:

1. **Caramelize Nuts:** In a skillet, cook 1 cup of nuts with 1/2 cup sugar over medium heat until the sugar melts and turns golden brown. Stir constantly to coat the nuts evenly. Cool completely.
2. **Blend:** Blend the cooled nuts and caramel in a food processor until you get a smooth paste.

Enjoy your **Tarte au Praliné**, a luxurious and nutty French dessert that's perfect for special occasions!

Gâteau de Mamie

Ingredients:

For the Cake:

- 1 1/2 cups (190 g) all-purpose flour
- 1 cup (200 g) granulated sugar
- 1/2 cup (115 g) unsalted butter, softened
- 3 large eggs
- 1/2 cup (120 ml) milk
- 1 teaspoon vanilla extract
- 2 teaspoons baking powder
- 1/4 teaspoon salt

For the Glaze (optional):

- 1/2 cup (60 g) powdered sugar
- 2-3 tablespoons milk or water
- 1 teaspoon vanilla extract

For Garnish (optional):

- Fresh berries
- Powdered sugar

Instructions:

1. Preheat Oven and Prepare the Pan:

- Preheat your oven to 350°F (175°C).
- Grease and flour an 8-inch (20 cm) round cake pan or line it with parchment paper.

2. Make the Cake Batter:

- In a mixing bowl, cream together the softened butter and sugar until light and fluffy.
- Beat in the eggs one at a time, making sure each is fully incorporated before adding the next. Mix in the vanilla extract.
- In another bowl, whisk together the flour, baking powder, and salt.
- Gradually add the dry ingredients to the butter mixture, alternating with the milk, beginning and ending with the dry ingredients. Mix until just combined.

3. Bake the Cake:

- Pour the batter into the prepared cake pan and smooth the top.

- Bake for 30-35 minutes, or until a toothpick inserted into the center comes out clean. Let cool in the pan for 10 minutes, then transfer to a wire rack to cool completely.

4. Prepare the Glaze (optional):

- In a small bowl, mix the powdered sugar with milk or water until smooth. Stir in the vanilla extract.
- Drizzle the glaze over the cooled cake.

5. Garnish and Serve:

- Garnish with fresh berries and a dusting of powdered sugar if desired.
- Slice and enjoy!

Gâteau de Mamie is simple yet delicious, perfect for a comforting treat with a cup of tea or coffee.

Pithiviers

Ingredients:

For the Puff Pastry:

- 1 package (about 14 oz or 400 g) frozen puff pastry, thawed (or homemade if preferred)

For the Almond Cream (Frangipane):

- 1/2 cup (115 g) unsalted butter, softened
- 1/2 cup (100 g) granulated sugar
- 1 cup (100 g) almond flour
- 2 large eggs
- 1 teaspoon vanilla extract
- 1 tablespoon all-purpose flour

For Assembly:

- 1 egg, beaten (for egg wash)
- 1 tablespoon slivered almonds (optional, for decoration)
- Powdered sugar (optional, for dusting)

Instructions:

1. Prepare the Almond Cream:

- In a mixing bowl, cream together the softened butter and granulated sugar until light and fluffy.
- Mix in the almond flour, eggs, vanilla extract, and flour until smooth.

2. Preheat Oven and Prepare the Pastry:

- Preheat your oven to 375°F (190°C).
- Roll out the puff pastry on a lightly floured surface. Cut two circles, each about 8-9 inches (20-23 cm) in diameter.

3. Assemble the Pithiviers:

- Place one pastry circle on a baking sheet lined with parchment paper.
- Spread the almond cream evenly over the pastry, leaving a small border around the edge.
- Brush the border with beaten egg.
- Place the second pastry circle on top, pressing the edges together to seal. Use a fork to crimp the edges.

- Decorate the top with a fork or a knife to create a pattern and lightly score the surface (optional).
- Brush the top with beaten egg and sprinkle with slivered almonds if using.

4. Bake the Pithiviers:

- Bake for 25-30 minutes, or until the pastry is golden brown and puffed.

5. Cool and Serve:

- Let the Pithiviers cool slightly before dusting with powdered sugar if desired.
- Slice and serve warm or at room temperature.

Enjoy your **Pithiviers**, a delightful and elegant French pastry that's perfect for any special occasion!

Gâteau au Chocolat Moelleux

Ingredients:

- 1/2 cup (115 g) unsalted butter, plus extra for greasing
- 1 cup (200 g) granulated sugar
- 1 cup (150 g) dark chocolate chips or chopped chocolate
- 3 large eggs
- 1/2 cup (60 g) all-purpose flour
- 1/4 cup (30 g) unsweetened cocoa powder
- 1/4 teaspoon salt
- 1/2 teaspoon vanilla extract

For Garnish (optional):

- Powdered sugar
- Fresh berries
- Whipped cream or vanilla ice cream

Instructions:

1. Preheat Oven and Prepare Pan:

- Preheat your oven to 350°F (175°C).
- Grease an 8-inch (20 cm) round cake pan and line the bottom with parchment paper.

2. Melt Chocolate and Butter:

- In a heatproof bowl, melt the chocolate and butter together over a pot of simmering water (double boiler) or in the microwave in short bursts. Stir until smooth and let cool slightly.

3. Mix Batter:

- In a mixing bowl, whisk the eggs and sugar until pale and thick.
- Stir in the melted chocolate mixture and vanilla extract.
- Sift together the flour, cocoa powder, and salt. Fold into the chocolate mixture until just combined.

4. Bake the Cake:

- Pour the batter into the prepared pan and smooth the top.
- Bake for 20-25 minutes. The cake should be set around the edges but still soft in the center. A toothpick inserted into the center should come out with a few moist crumbs.

5. Cool and Serve:

- Let the cake cool in the pan for 10 minutes before transferring to a wire rack to cool completely.
- Dust with powdered sugar and garnish with fresh berries and whipped cream or vanilla ice cream if desired.

Enjoy your **Gâteau au Chocolat Moelleux**, a decadent and indulgent chocolate treat with a luscious, molten center!

Tarte aux Poires

Ingredients:

For the Tart Crust:

- 1 1/4 cups (160 g) all-purpose flour
- 1/2 cup (115 g) unsalted butter, cold and cut into cubes
- 1/4 cup (50 g) granulated sugar
- 1/4 teaspoon salt
- 1 large egg yolk
- 1-2 tablespoons ice water

For the Almond Cream (Frangipane):

- 1/2 cup (115 g) unsalted butter, softened
- 1/2 cup (100 g) granulated sugar
- 1 cup (100 g) almond flour
- 2 large eggs
- 1 teaspoon vanilla extract
- 1 tablespoon all-purpose flour

For the Pear Topping:

- 3-4 ripe pears (such as Bosc or Anjou)
- 1 tablespoon lemon juice
- 2 tablespoons apricot jam or preserves (optional, for glazing)

Instructions:

1. Prepare the Tart Crust:

- In a bowl or food processor, combine the flour, sugar, and salt. Add the cold butter and mix until the mixture resembles coarse crumbs.
- Stir in the egg yolk and mix until the dough just comes together. Add ice water if needed.
- Shape the dough into a disk, wrap in plastic wrap, and refrigerate for at least 30 minutes.

2. Preheat Oven and Prepare the Pan:

- Preheat your oven to 375°F (190°C).
- Roll out the chilled dough on a lightly floured surface and fit it into a 9-inch (23 cm) tart pan. Trim any excess dough.

3. Prepare the Almond Cream:

- In a mixing bowl, cream together the softened butter and sugar until light and fluffy.

- Mix in the almond flour, eggs, vanilla extract, and flour until smooth.

4. Assemble the Tart:

- Spread the almond cream evenly over the prepared tart shell.
- Peel, core, and slice the pears. Arrange the pear slices on top of the almond cream in a decorative pattern.

5. Bake the Tart:

- Bake for 30-35 minutes, or until the tart is golden brown and the almond cream is set. A knife inserted into the filling should come out clean.

6. Glaze and Serve:

- If desired, warm the apricot jam and brush it over the baked pears for a shiny finish.
- Allow the tart to cool before slicing.

Enjoy your **Tarte aux Poires**, a delicious and refined dessert perfect for any occasion!

Kouign-Amann

Ingredients:

For the Dough:

- 2 1/4 teaspoons (7 g) active dry yeast
- 1/4 cup (60 ml) warm water (110°F/45°C)
- 3/4 cup (180 ml) whole milk, warm
- 1/4 cup (50 g) granulated sugar
- 3 1/2 cups (440 g) all-purpose flour
- 1 teaspoon salt
- 1/2 cup (115 g) unsalted butter, softened

For the Butter and Sugar Layer:

- 1 cup (230 g) unsalted butter, cold and cut into small pieces
- 1 cup (200 g) granulated sugar

For the Caramelized Sugar:

- 1/2 cup (100 g) granulated sugar

Instructions:

1. Prepare the Dough:

- In a small bowl, dissolve the yeast in warm water and let it sit for about 5 minutes until frothy.
- In a large bowl, combine the warm milk, sugar, and yeast mixture. Add the flour and salt, then mix until a dough forms.
- Knead the dough on a lightly floured surface for about 5-7 minutes, until smooth and elastic.
- Place the dough in a lightly greased bowl, cover with a damp cloth or plastic wrap, and let it rise in a warm place for about 1 hour or until doubled in size.

2. Prepare the Butter Layer:

- Place the cold butter between two sheets of parchment paper. Use a rolling pin to flatten it into a rectangle about 1/2 inch (1.25 cm) thick. Chill until firm.

3. Laminate the Dough:

- On a lightly floured surface, roll out the dough into a rectangle, about 1/2 inch (1.25 cm) thick.

- Place the chilled butter rectangle in the center of the dough. Fold the dough over the butter, sealing the edges.
- Roll out the dough into a larger rectangle, then fold it into thirds (like a letter). Chill for 30 minutes.
- Repeat the rolling and folding process 2 more times, chilling the dough between each fold.

4. Shape the Kouign-Amann:

- Preheat your oven to 400°F (200°C). Grease a 9-inch (23 cm) round cake pan.
- Roll out the dough into a rectangle about 1/4 inch (0.6 cm) thick. Sprinkle the sugar evenly over the dough.
- Fold the dough into thirds, then cut it into squares. Arrange the squares in the prepared pan, overlapping them slightly.
- Sprinkle the top with additional sugar.

5. Bake the Kouign-Amann:

- Bake for 30-35 minutes, or until golden brown and caramelized. A toothpick inserted into the center should come out clean.

6. Cool and Serve:

- Let the Kouign-Amann cool in the pan for 10 minutes before transferring to a wire rack to cool completely.

Enjoy your **Kouign-Amann**, a luscious and flaky pastry with a delightful caramelized crust!

Gâteau aux Pommes

Ingredients:

For the Cake:

- 1 1/2 cups (190 g) all-purpose flour
- 1 cup (200 g) granulated sugar
- 1/2 cup (115 g) unsalted butter, softened
- 2 large eggs
- 1/2 cup (120 ml) milk
- 1 teaspoon vanilla extract
- 1 1/2 teaspoons baking powder
- 1/4 teaspoon salt
- 1 teaspoon ground cinnamon (optional)

For the Apples:

- 3-4 medium apples (such as Granny Smith or Honeycrisp)
- 1 tablespoon lemon juice
- 2 tablespoons granulated sugar
- 1/2 teaspoon ground cinnamon

For Garnish (optional):

- Powdered sugar
- Whipped cream or vanilla ice cream

Instructions:

1. Preheat Oven and Prepare Pan:

- Preheat your oven to 350°F (175°C).
- Grease and flour a 9-inch (23 cm) round cake pan or line it with parchment paper.

2. Prepare the Apples:

- Peel, core, and slice the apples thinly. Toss with lemon juice, sugar, and cinnamon. Set aside.

3. Make the Cake Batter:

- In a mixing bowl, cream together the softened butter and granulated sugar until light and fluffy.
- Beat in the eggs one at a time, then mix in the vanilla extract.
- In another bowl, whisk together the flour, baking powder, salt, and cinnamon.

- Gradually add the dry ingredients to the butter mixture, alternating with the milk, and mix until just combined.

4. Assemble the Cake:

- Pour the batter into the prepared pan and smooth the top.
- Arrange the apple slices evenly over the batter, slightly pressing them in.

5. Bake the Cake:

- Bake for 35-40 minutes, or until a toothpick inserted into the center comes out clean and the cake is golden brown.

6. Cool and Serve:

- Allow the cake to cool in the pan for 10 minutes, then transfer to a wire rack to cool completely.
- Dust with powdered sugar and serve with whipped cream or vanilla ice cream if desired.

Enjoy your **Gâteau aux Pommes**, a comforting and delicious apple cake that's perfect for any occasion!

Gâteau au Citron

Ingredients:

For the Cake:

- 1 1/2 cups (190 g) all-purpose flour
- 1 cup (200 g) granulated sugar
- 1/2 cup (115 g) unsalted butter, softened
- 2 large eggs
- 1/2 cup (120 ml) milk
- 1/4 cup (60 ml) freshly squeezed lemon juice (about 1-2 lemons)
- Zest of 2 lemons
- 1 1/2 teaspoons baking powder
- 1/4 teaspoon salt

For the Lemon Glaze:

- 1 cup (120 g) powdered sugar
- 2-3 tablespoons freshly squeezed lemon juice

For Garnish (optional):

- Lemon zest
- Fresh berries

Instructions:

1. Preheat Oven and Prepare Pan:

- Preheat your oven to 350°F (175°C).
- Grease and flour an 8-inch (20 cm) round cake pan or line it with parchment paper.

2. Make the Cake Batter:

- In a mixing bowl, cream together the softened butter and granulated sugar until light and fluffy.
- Beat in the eggs one at a time, ensuring each is fully incorporated before adding the next.
- Mix in the lemon zest and lemon juice.
- In another bowl, whisk together the flour, baking powder, and salt.
- Gradually add the dry ingredients to the butter mixture, alternating with the milk, and mix until just combined.

3. Bake the Cake:

- Pour the batter into the prepared cake pan and smooth the top.
- Bake for 25-30 minutes, or until a toothpick inserted into the center comes out clean and the cake is golden brown.

4. Prepare the Lemon Glaze:

- In a small bowl, mix the powdered sugar with lemon juice until smooth. Adjust the consistency with more lemon juice or powdered sugar if needed.

5. Cool and Glaze:

- Allow the cake to cool in the pan for 10 minutes, then transfer to a wire rack to cool completely.
- Drizzle the lemon glaze over the cooled cake.

6. Garnish and Serve:

- Garnish with additional lemon zest and fresh berries if desired.
- Serve and enjoy!

Gâteau au Citron is a wonderfully bright and zesty cake that's perfect for bringing a touch of sunshine to your dessert table. Enjoy this delightful French treat!

Tarte au Caramel

Ingredients:

For the Tart Crust:

- 1 1/4 cups (160 g) all-purpose flour
- 1/2 cup (115 g) unsalted butter, cold and cut into cubes
- 1/4 cup (50 g) granulated sugar
- 1/4 teaspoon salt
- 1 large egg yolk
- 1-2 tablespoons ice water

For the Caramel Filling:

- 1 cup (200 g) granulated sugar
- 6 tablespoons (85 g) unsalted butter, cut into pieces
- 1/2 cup (120 ml) heavy cream
- 1/4 cup (60 ml) light corn syrup (or golden syrup)
- 1/4 teaspoon sea salt (optional, for a salted caramel version)

For Garnish (optional):

- Sea salt flakes
- Whipped cream

Instructions:

1. Prepare the Tart Crust:

- In a bowl or food processor, combine the flour, sugar, and salt. Add the cold butter and mix until the mixture resembles coarse crumbs.
- Stir in the egg yolk and mix until the dough just comes together. Add ice water if needed.
- Shape the dough into a disk, wrap in plastic wrap, and refrigerate for at least 30 minutes.

2. Preheat Oven and Prepare the Pan:

- Preheat your oven to 375°F (190°C).
- Roll out the chilled dough on a lightly floured surface and fit it into a 9-inch (23 cm) tart pan. Trim any excess dough.

3. Blind Bake the Tart Crust:

- Line the tart shell with parchment paper and fill with pie weights or dried beans.
- Bake for 15 minutes, then remove the parchment and weights. Bake for an additional 5-7 minutes until golden brown. Let cool completely.

4. Prepare the Caramel Filling:

- In a medium saucepan, heat the sugar over medium heat, stirring constantly until it melts and turns a deep amber color. Be careful not to burn it.
- Remove from heat and quickly stir in the butter until fully incorporated.
- Gradually add the heavy cream, stirring continuously (the mixture will bubble vigorously). Stir in the corn syrup and salt if using.
- Return the saucepan to low heat and cook for an additional 1-2 minutes, stirring constantly, until the caramel is smooth and slightly thickened.

5. Assemble the Tart:

- Pour the caramel filling into the cooled tart shell, spreading it evenly with a spatula.
- Allow the caramel to set at room temperature for about 1 hour, or until firm.

6. Garnish and Serve:

- If desired, sprinkle with sea salt flakes before serving.
- Garnish with whipped cream if desired.

Enjoy your **Tarte au Caramel**, a rich and decadent dessert that combines a buttery tart crust with smooth, sweet caramel filling!

Gâteau de Voyage

Ingredients:

For the Cake:

- 1 1/2 cups (190 g) all-purpose flour
- 1 cup (200 g) granulated sugar
- 1/2 cup (115 g) unsalted butter, softened
- 3 large eggs
- 1/2 cup (120 ml) milk
- 1 teaspoon vanilla extract
- 1 1/2 teaspoons baking powder
- 1/4 teaspoon salt

Optional Add-ins (for extra flavor):

- 1/2 cup (80 g) chopped nuts (such as almonds or walnuts)
- 1/2 cup (75 g) dried fruit (such as raisins or cranberries)
- 1 teaspoon ground cinnamon or other spices

Instructions:

1. Preheat Oven and Prepare Pan:

- Preheat your oven to 350°F (175°C).
- Grease and flour a 9-inch (23 cm) loaf pan or line it with parchment paper.

2. Make the Cake Batter:

- In a mixing bowl, cream together the softened butter and granulated sugar until light and fluffy.
- Beat in the eggs one at a time, ensuring each is fully incorporated before adding the next.
- Mix in the vanilla extract.
- In another bowl, whisk together the flour, baking powder, and salt.
- Gradually add the dry ingredients to the butter mixture, alternating with the milk, and mix until just combined.

3. Optional Add-ins:

- If using nuts, dried fruit, or spices, fold them into the batter now.

4. Bake the Cake:

- Pour the batter into the prepared pan and smooth the top.

- Bake for 45-55 minutes, or until a toothpick inserted into the center comes out clean and the cake is golden brown.

5. Cool and Serve:

- Allow the cake to cool in the pan for about 10 minutes, then transfer to a wire rack to cool completely.
- Slice and serve.

Gâteau de Voyage is perfect for taking along on a trip, enjoying as a snack with tea or coffee, or sharing with friends and family. Its simple, yet delicious flavors make it a versatile and enduring classic in French baking.

Bûche Pralinée

Ingredients:

For the Sponge Cake (Génoise):

- 4 large eggs
- 1 cup (200 g) granulated sugar
- 1 cup (125 g) all-purpose flour
- 1/4 cup (60 ml) milk
- 1/4 cup (60 g) unsalted butter, melted
- 1 teaspoon vanilla extract

For the Praline Filling:

- 1 cup (200 g) praline paste (store-bought or homemade)
- 1 cup (240 ml) heavy cream
- 1/2 cup (115 g) unsalted butter, softened

For the Chocolate Glaze:

- 1/2 cup (120 ml) heavy cream
- 4 oz (115 g) dark chocolate, chopped
- 1 tablespoon unsalted butter

For Garnish (optional):

- Praline pieces
- Fresh berries
- Mint leaves

Instructions:

1. Prepare the Sponge Cake:

- Preheat your oven to 350°F (175°C). Line a 10x15 inch (25x38 cm) baking sheet with parchment paper.
- In a mixing bowl, beat the eggs and sugar until thick and pale.
- Fold in the flour gently until just combined.
- In a separate bowl, mix the milk, melted butter, and vanilla extract. Fold this mixture into the batter.
- Pour the batter onto the prepared baking sheet and spread evenly.
- Bake for 10-12 minutes, or until the cake is lightly golden and springs back when touched.
- Turn the cake out onto a clean towel dusted with powdered sugar. Remove the parchment paper and roll the cake up with the towel to cool.

2. Prepare the Praline Filling:

- In a bowl, beat the heavy cream until soft peaks form.
- Fold in the praline paste and softened butter until smooth.

3. Assemble the Bûche:

- Unroll the cooled sponge cake and spread the praline filling evenly over the surface.
- Roll the cake back up, using the towel to help shape it into a log. Place seam side down on a serving platter.

4. Prepare the Chocolate Glaze:

- Heat the heavy cream in a saucepan until just simmering. Pour over the chopped chocolate in a heatproof bowl.
- Let sit for a few minutes, then stir until smooth. Stir in the butter until glossy.

5. Glaze the Bûche:

- Pour the chocolate glaze over the rolled cake, smoothing it with a spatula.
- Chill the cake in the refrigerator for at least 1 hour to set.

6. Garnish and Serve:

- Decorate with praline pieces, fresh berries, or mint leaves if desired.
- Slice and serve chilled.

Enjoy your **Bûche Pralinée**, a festive and elegant dessert that brings a touch of French sophistication to your holiday celebrations!

Gâteau Opéra

Ingredients:

For the Joconde Sponge Cake:

- 1/2 cup (60 g) almond flour
- 1/2 cup (65 g) all-purpose flour
- 1/2 cup (100 g) granulated sugar
- 4 large eggs
- 2 large egg whites
- 2 tablespoons (30 g) unsalted butter, melted
- 1/4 teaspoon salt

For the Coffee Syrup:

- 1/2 cup (120 ml) brewed espresso or strong coffee
- 1/4 cup (50 g) granulated sugar

For the Coffee Buttercream:

- 1/2 cup (115 g) unsalted butter, softened
- 1/2 cup (100 g) granulated sugar
- 1/4 cup (60 ml) brewed espresso or strong coffee
- 2 large egg yolks
- 1/4 teaspoon vanilla extract

For the Chocolate Ganache:

- 1 cup (240 ml) heavy cream
- 8 oz (225 g) dark chocolate, chopped
- 1 tablespoon unsalted butter

For Assembly:

- Cocoa powder or chocolate shavings (optional, for decoration)

Instructions:

1. Prepare the Joconde Sponge Cake:

- Preheat your oven to 375°F (190°C). Line a 12x16 inch (30x40 cm) baking sheet with parchment paper.
- In a bowl, whisk together the almond flour, all-purpose flour, and 1/4 cup (50 g) of sugar. Set aside.
- In another bowl, beat the eggs and remaining sugar until thick and pale.

- Fold the dry ingredients into the egg mixture, then fold in the melted butter.
- In a separate bowl, whip the egg whites with a pinch of salt until stiff peaks form. Gently fold the egg whites into the batter.
- Spread the batter evenly on the prepared baking sheet and bake for 8-10 minutes, or until golden and springy. Let cool completely.

2. Make the Coffee Syrup:

- Combine the espresso or coffee with sugar in a small saucepan. Heat until the sugar is dissolved. Let cool.

3. Prepare the Coffee Buttercream:

- In a heatproof bowl, whisk the egg yolks and sugar over a pot of simmering water until thick and pale.
- Remove from heat and beat in the brewed coffee and vanilla extract.
- Allow the mixture to cool slightly, then beat in the softened butter until smooth and creamy.

4. Prepare the Chocolate Ganache:

- Heat the heavy cream until just simmering. Pour over the chopped chocolate in a heatproof bowl. Let sit for a few minutes, then stir until smooth. Stir in the butter until glossy.

5. Assemble the Gâteau Opéra:

- Trim the edges of the cooled sponge cake and cut it into 3 equal rectangles.
- Place one layer of sponge cake on a serving platter. Brush with coffee syrup.
- Spread a layer of coffee buttercream over the sponge.
- Place the second layer of sponge on top, brush with coffee syrup, and spread a layer of chocolate ganache.
- Place the third layer of sponge on top, brush with coffee syrup, and spread a final layer of coffee buttercream.
- Refrigerate for at least 2 hours to set.

6. Finish and Serve:

- Once set, pour the remaining chocolate ganache over the top layer and smooth it out.
- Decorate with cocoa powder or chocolate shavings if desired.
- Slice and serve chilled.

Enjoy your **Gâteau Opéra**, a beautifully layered and flavorful cake that's perfect for special occasions or a luxurious treat!

Gâteau au Miel

Ingredients:

For the Cake:

- 1 1/2 cups (190 g) all-purpose flour
- 1 cup (200 g) granulated sugar
- 1/2 cup (115 g) unsalted butter, softened
- 1/2 cup (120 ml) honey
- 2 large eggs
- 1/2 cup (120 ml) milk
- 1 1/2 teaspoons baking powder
- 1/2 teaspoon baking soda
- 1/4 teaspoon salt
- 1 teaspoon vanilla extract

For the Honey Glaze (optional):

- 1/4 cup (60 ml) honey
- 1 tablespoon water

For Garnish (optional):

- Chopped nuts (such as walnuts or almonds)
- Fresh fruit (such as berries or apple slices)
- Powdered sugar

Instructions:

1. Preheat Oven and Prepare Pan:

- Preheat your oven to 350°F (175°C).
- Grease and flour an 8-inch (20 cm) round cake pan or line it with parchment paper.

2. Make the Cake Batter:

- In a mixing bowl, cream together the softened butter and granulated sugar until light and fluffy.
- Beat in the eggs one at a time, ensuring each is fully incorporated before adding the next.
- Mix in the honey and vanilla extract until smooth.
- In another bowl, whisk together the flour, baking powder, baking soda, and salt.
- Gradually add the dry ingredients to the wet mixture, alternating with the milk, and mix until just combined.

3. Bake the Cake:

- Pour the batter into the prepared pan and smooth the top.
- Bake for 30-35 minutes, or until a toothpick inserted into the center comes out clean and the cake is golden brown.
- Allow the cake to cool in the pan for 10 minutes, then transfer to a wire rack to cool completely.

4. Prepare the Honey Glaze (optional):

- In a small saucepan, heat the honey and water over low heat until warmed and slightly thinned.
- Brush the glaze over the cooled cake for a glossy finish.

5. Garnish and Serve:

- Garnish with chopped nuts, fresh fruit, or a dusting of powdered sugar if desired.
- Serve and enjoy!

Gâteau au Miel is a moist and flavorful cake that highlights the natural sweetness of honey, making it a comforting and satisfying dessert for any occasion.

Tarte au Miel

Ingredients:

For the Tart Crust:

- 1 1/4 cups (160 g) all-purpose flour
- 1/2 cup (115 g) unsalted butter, cold and cut into cubes
- 1/4 cup (50 g) granulated sugar
- 1/4 teaspoon salt
- 1 large egg yolk
- 1-2 tablespoons ice water (as needed)

For the Honey Filling:

- 1 cup (240 ml) heavy cream
- 1/2 cup (120 ml) honey
- 1/2 cup (100 g) granulated sugar
- 4 large egg yolks
- 1 tablespoon unsalted butter
- 1 teaspoon vanilla extract

For Garnish (optional):

- Fresh herbs (such as thyme or mint)
- Toasted nuts (such as almonds or hazelnuts)
- Edible flowers

Instructions:

1. Prepare the Tart Crust:

- In a food processor, combine the flour, sugar, and salt. Add the cold butter and pulse until the mixture resembles coarse crumbs.
- Add the egg yolk and pulse to combine. Gradually add ice water, 1 tablespoon at a time, until the dough just comes together.
- Turn the dough out onto a lightly floured surface and gently knead it into a disk Wrap in plastic wrap and refrigerate for at least 30 minutes.

2. Preheat Oven and Prepare the Pan:

- Preheat your oven to 375°F (190°C).
- On a lightly floured surface, roll out the chilled dough to fit a 9-inch (23 cm) tart pan with a removable bottom. Press the dough into the pan and trim any excess. Prick the bottom with a fork.

3. Blind Bake the Tart Crust:

- Line the tart shell with parchment paper and fill with pie weights or dried beans.
- Bake for 15 minutes, then remove the parchment and weights. Bake for an additional 5-7 minutes, or until the crust is lightly golden. Let cool completely.

4. Prepare the Honey Filling:

- In a saucepan, combine the heavy cream, honey, and sugar. Heat over medium heat until the sugar is dissolved and the mixture is warmed (do not boil).
- In a heatproof bowl, whisk the egg yolks. Gradually add the warm cream mixture to the egg yolks, whisking constantly.
- Return the mixture to the saucepan and cook over low heat, stirring constantly, until the filling thickens slightly (it should coat the back of a spoon). Do not let it boil.
- Remove from heat and stir in the butter and vanilla extract until smooth.

5. Assemble the Tart:

- Pour the honey filling into the cooled tart crust and smooth the top.
- Refrigerate the tart for at least 2 hours, or until the filling is set.

6. Garnish and Serve:

- Garnish with fresh herbs, toasted nuts, or edible flowers if desired.
- Serve chilled or at room temperature.

Enjoy your **Tarte au Miel**, a sweet and refined dessert that beautifully showcases the rich flavor of honey!

Tarte Normande

Ingredients:

For the Pastry Crust:

- 1 1/4 cups (160 g) all-purpose flour
- 1/2 cup (115 g) unsalted butter, cold and cut into cubes
- 1/4 cup (50 g) granulated sugar
- 1/4 teaspoon salt
- 1 large egg yolk
- 1-2 tablespoons ice water (as needed)

For the Apple Filling:

- 4-5 medium apples (such as Granny Smith or Braeburn), peeled, cored, and thinly sliced
- 2 tablespoons (30 g) unsalted butter
- 1/4 cup (50 g) granulated sugar
- 1 teaspoon ground cinnamon

For the Custard Filling:

- 1 cup (240 ml) heavy cream
- 1/2 cup (100 g) granulated sugar
- 2 large eggs
- 1 teaspoon vanilla extract
- 2 tablespoons (30 g) all-purpose flour

For Garnish (optional):

- Powdered sugar
- Fresh whipped cream or vanilla ice cream

Instructions:

1. Prepare the Pastry Crust:

- In a food processor, combine the flour, sugar, and salt. Add the cold butter and pulse until the mixture resembles coarse crumbs.
- Add the egg yolk and pulse to combine. Gradually add ice water, 1 tablespoon at a time, until the dough just comes together.
- Turn the dough out onto a lightly floured surface and gently knead it into a disk. Wrap in plastic wrap and refrigerate for at least 30 minutes.

2. Preheat Oven and Prepare the Pan:

- Preheat your oven to 375°F (190°C).
- On a lightly floured surface, roll out the chilled dough to fit a 9-inch (23 cm) tart pan with a removable bottom. Press the dough into the pan and trim any excess. Prick the bottom with a fork.

3. Blind Bake the Tart Crust:

- Line the tart shell with parchment paper and fill with pie weights or dried beans.
- Bake for 15 minutes, then remove the parchment and weights. Bake for an additional 5-7 minutes, or until the crust is lightly golden. Let cool slightly.

4. Prepare the Apple Filling:

- In a skillet, melt the butter over medium heat. Add the apple slices and cook until they start to soften, about 5 minutes.
- Sprinkle with sugar and cinnamon, and cook for another 5 minutes, until the apples are tender and caramelized. Remove from heat and let cool.

5. Prepare the Custard Filling:

- In a mixing bowl, whisk together the heavy cream, sugar, eggs, vanilla extract, and flour until smooth.

6. Assemble the Tarte Normande:

- Spread the cooked apples evenly over the partially baked tart crust.
- Pour the custard filling over the apples, filling the tart to the top.

7. Bake the Tart:

- Bake the tart for 30-35 minutes, or until the custard is set and the top is golden brown.
- Allow the tart to cool in the pan for 10 minutes, then transfer to a wire rack to cool completely.

8. Garnish and Serve:

- Dust with powdered sugar if desired.
- Serve warm or at room temperature with fresh whipped cream or vanilla ice cream.

Enjoy your **Tarte Normande**, a classic French dessert that combines the tartness of apples with a rich, creamy custard filling!

Gâteau à la Crème

Ingredients:

For the Cake:

- 1 1/2 cups (190 g) all-purpose flour
- 1 cup (200 g) granulated sugar
- 1/2 cup (115 g) unsalted butter, softened
- 1/2 cup (120 ml) milk
- 3 large eggs
- 1 1/2 teaspoons baking powder
- 1/4 teaspoon salt
- 1 teaspoon vanilla extract

For the Cream Filling:

- 1 cup (240 ml) heavy cream
- 1/4 cup (50 g) granulated sugar
- 1 teaspoon vanilla extract

For the Optional Filling (e.g., fruit, jam):

- 1/2 cup (120 ml) fruit jam or fresh fruit (such as berries or sliced peaches)

For the Frosting:

- 1 cup (240 ml) heavy cream
- 2 tablespoons granulated sugar
- 1 teaspoon vanilla extract

For Garnish (optional):

- Fresh berries
- Mint leaves
- Shredded coconut or chocolate shavings

Instructions:

1. Preheat Oven and Prepare the Pan:

- Preheat your oven to 350°F (175°C).
- Grease and flour two 8-inch (20 cm) round cake pans or line them with parchment paper.

2. Make the Cake Batter:

- In a mixing bowl, cream together the softened butter and granulated sugar until light and fluffy.
- Beat in the eggs one at a time, ensuring each is fully incorporated before adding the next.
- Mix in the vanilla extract.
- In another bowl, whisk together the flour, baking powder, and salt.
- Gradually add the dry ingredients to the butter mixture, alternating with the milk, and mix until just combined.

3. Bake the Cake:

- Divide the batter evenly between the prepared pans and smooth the tops.
- Bake for 25-30 minutes, or until a toothpick inserted into the center comes out clean and the cakes are golden brown.
- Allow the cakes to cool in the pans for 10 minutes, then transfer to a wire rack to cool completely.

4. Prepare the Cream Filling:

- In a mixing bowl, whip the heavy cream, sugar, and vanilla extract until soft peaks form.

5. Assemble the Cake:

- If desired, spread a layer of fruit jam or fresh fruit on top of one of the cake layers.
- Spread a generous layer of whipped cream over the jam or fruit.
- Place the second cake layer on top.

6. Prepare the Frosting:

- In a mixing bowl, whip the heavy cream, sugar, and vanilla extract until stiff peaks form.

7. Frost the Cake:

- Spread the whipped cream frosting evenly over the top and sides of the cake.
- Garnish with fresh berries, mint leaves, shredded coconut, or chocolate shavings if desired.

8. Chill and Serve:

- Refrigerate the cake for at least 1 hour to allow the flavors to meld and the cream to set.
- Slice and serve chilled.

Enjoy your **Gâteau à la Crème**, a light and delicious cake that's perfect for any occasion or simply to indulge in a creamy treat!

www.ingramcontent.com/pod-product-compliance
Lightning Source LLC
LaVergne TN
LVHW081607060526
838201LV00054B/2111